The Life and Times of a
One-Armed Surgeon

By Morris A. Robbins, M.D.

Annotated by
Dorothy Talavera

The Life and Times of a One-Armed Surgeon

©2020 Dorothy Robbins Talavera

print ISBN: 978-1-09835-400-8

Foreword

My father, Morris A. Robbins, M.D., was a uniquely special man who achieved his life's dream of becoming a surgeon despite the loss of his left arm in a terrible accident. He earned the professional respect of colleagues and patients. Even today, his patients talk about him. In a recent conversation with a group of people that included a former patient., someone asked "Didn't you feel uncomfortable being operated on by a doctor with only one arm?" The former patient replied, "No. Everybody knew he was the best."

Doc began writing an autobiography in 1993, recording his memories, struggles, and thoughts on his profession. What he wrote about himself is very clinical and humble, with no self-aggrandizement. His objective was to inspire and instruct. Thanks to the invention of word processing technology, he was able to write, edit and reproduce his book over and over, typing by tapping the keys with one finger of his deformed right hand. He gave copies to family and friends as a gift.

After his death, I discovered a cabinet full of papers that were important enough to him that he kept them for the rest of his life. These documents support and add voice to what he had written, and shed light on the story. I have taken the liberty of supplementing my father's words with excerpts from these documents, photos from the family album, letters, newspaper clippings, explanations and comments from people who knew him.

Doc chronicles his life, the growth of his profession, and developments in medical practice and hospitals during his lifetime, courageously giving an honest assessment of the changing situation as he sees it. He is candid, but uncomplaining, about the physical, emotional and organizational obstacles he faced.

Dorothy Robbins Talavera
Delanco, New Jersey
talaveradorothy@gmail.com
© 2020

Contents

Chapter 1
THE REASON FOR WRITING THIS BOOK

By nature, I am too modest to tell the story of my life. If I had not had a devastating accident in early manhood, overcome frustrating disability and proceeded on the course that I had envisioned before the accident, there would be nothing of interest to the general reader. The real purpose of this book is to attempt to inspire faith in the reader's innate ability to fulfill the role assigned by his Creator and to instruct, by example, in the methods of attainment. Whether or not the reader has a physical handicap, the observations and experiences herein should encourage and guide his journey along the road of life.

I have been practicing medicine fifty years. Many patients have been curious about my physical appearance. Some are afraid to inquire, others politely approach the subject and a few are downright rude. This book is the result of conversations concerning myself and my patients' personal medical problems. The one-armed surgeon is the central theme, but some recent history of medical practice is presented for young physicians and their patients, and as nostalgia for the oldsters.

The first section tells of an old-fashioned childhood spent in a small rural community. This is partly for historical Americana because suburbia has replaced such communities in many parts of the country. More importantly, they illustrate that success does not elude the country bumpkin if he broadens his mind and believes he can handle himself in the big-time.

The middle section describes unusually rough times in my life. A devastating accident in adolescence left me permanently maimed. I tell how I handled the obstacles which sometimes seemed overwhelming. By these means I hope to encourage others, who may feel uncertain or inferior, to push ahead with their chosen careers without compromising out of fear or advice from others.

The last section describes my practice, for entertainment, history, description of my special adaptations, and plain language commentary on my specialty of orthopedic surgery. People want medical science explained to them in terms they understand. I hope medical students and young physicians will appreciate the historic details and be encouraged to uphold the dignity of the profession. I admit that some of the advice is a bit dated and unacceptable to the present generation of orthopedists, since time marches on.

The special anatomy of this narrative is the human hand. If one is told that he has the hands of a surgeon, he is being complemented on his dexterity and expertise. To be labeled a good surgeon when his hands are deformed or, as in my case, one is deformed and the other is absent, is a super compliment. This situation is so foreign to the image of a surgeon that it calls for careful documentation to give it credibility. Even doctors will find this story hard to believe.

Since this narrative was written over a period of fifteen years there is a large portion in the present tense, like a diary. This should be more interesting and thought-provoking than dull descriptions of past events.

Chapter 2

THE HUMAN HAND

Since my entire adult life and career has been influenced by my hand injuries, I believe a treatise on the human hand is in order to make the autobiography meaningful.

The intact human hand is useful regardless of the ability of the brain to control it. It has been described as a direct extension of the brain. Biologists agree that the hand, especially the thumb, physically distinguishes man from the other primates. In all mammals, the end structure of the upper or forward extremities is especially adapted to the living habits and requirements of the organism.

Some animals, such as raccoons and squirrels, sit on their haunches and oppose the palms of their front paws to hold their food while they tear it apart with their teeth. They use the same mechanism to walk, run or climb. Their "finger nails" are cone-shaped spikes which are used for traction, ripping and defense. Their thumbs are not so important or well-developed as in man because these animals do not have the mentality to demand other manual functions. The smaller monkeys have long fingers and human type nails, but their thumbs are short and will not oppose each finger, as in man. In all primates the hands do what they are supposed to do, but they are not developed any farther than the brain of each species demands. Even the ape and chimpanzee, human as they seem, have limited thumb structure.

The normal human hand, in contrast, is constructed so that intelligent activities are possible inasmuch as the individual's brain is capable of directing it. Young minds control developing and growing hands appropriately. Mentally retarded people[1] usually possess all the dexterity their minds can handle. Regardless of talent, hands testify that they are human by their structure.

---

1   Some of the terminology Doc uses is different from what is common today. It is hoped the reader will focus on the content, rather than dwelling on dated language.

It is unfortunate that not all hands are perfect. Some babies are born with defects which limit further development of manipulation or sensation. Even if the mind is agile, expression through malformed hands is unconventional, inconvenient and sometimes impossible. In spite of this, many individuals who have never had the experience of normal hands adapt other parts of their bodies and invent methods of carrying out their mental directions. Their private lives are fairly adequate.

The real difficulty is that normal people never quite accept physically abnormal ones as equals, and have a tendency to avoid them, minimize contacts, compartmentalize them as misfits or overprotect them. Congenitally handicapped children, in their constant frustration, are prone to antisocial tendencies in attitude and behavior. In spite of modern reconstructive hand surgery, they will never be normal.

The previously normal person who loses parts and functions of his hands through injury or disease is devastated. He has hand sense, or image in his mind, with normal experiences and development. Injury or disease is sudden, and the individual must quickly adjust to the new situation, for which he is neither forewarned nor prepared. It is also permanent. The degree of emotional shock and physical handicap depends upon the extent and location of the injury. The age at which the mishap occurs is also important, as are education, training and experience.

Childhood handicaps are easier to handle than those acquired in adulthood, where life patterns already have become well established. Maimed children and adults start out the same as congenitally defective children, but they know what they have lost and tend to be highly frustrated for a while. They can educate and train themselves to cope with their handicap, and are usually somewhat successful. Although admired, they still may be treated unwisely by their associates. The smaller and less noticeable the defect is, the less discomfort and difficulty will be experienced. How many times have you known a person for years, on a casual basis, without noticing a missing finger or an artificial leg?

Younger adults are much more devastated by partial or complete limb loss, especially of the upper extremities, than are children. They have to learn all over again, often changing their occupation, hobbies and daily living habits. They may lose some of their friends through embarrassment or inability to participate in former mutual activities. Today, many newly disabled adults receive financial compensation which may lessen their ambition to improve themselves.

Proportionately, more adults than children suffer sudden loss of manual dexterity. Strokes are common, and they usually ruin a whole hand. The younger the stroke victim, the less certain is his future. In seniors the stroke often comes in the twilight years and has much less impact upon the already slowed-down individual.

I experienced a sudden, overwhelming, traumatic amputation of my left arm just below the elbow and severe loss of form and function of my remaining right hand, in late adolescence. I want to relate my experiences in rehabilitation, training and occupation. Some of these led to triumph and others to disappointment or defeat.

I know a lot about public attitudes toward the crippled and maimed from more than a half century of experience in a world which suddenly became hostile when I graduated from high school. I want to help the handicapped and guide normal people in understanding them.

In my particular case, the biological relationship between the brain and hand has been artificially reversed because of the accident. My brain, thankfully, is more highly developed and functional than my remaining hand. Thus, the emotional price has been frustration and self-consciousness. I have been able to avoid self-pity. Salvation has come through my natural and educated ingenuity—-or just plain inventiveness. Without this there would be no material or reason for an autobiography.

Chapter 3

THE OLD FARM

The Robbins farm; farm machinery fascinated young Morris

My life began on a farm, where I lived for eight years. Since the farm life partially molded my personality and abilities, I want to share it, especially since such environment is becoming rare in these parts.

My great-grandfather, Aaron Robbins, moved his family from Rancocas, New Jersey, to a forty acre, sandy-soiled farm near Jacksonville,

New Jersey, in 1850. His father, John, supposedly came from Britain[2]. Aaron served with the New Jersey Volunteers in the Civil War and was wounded twice. His cane, saddle, uniform markings and military papers are preserved. After the war he ran the post office in Jacksonville.

Clarence, Sarah and Morris Robbins, December 1917

My father, Clarence Rhubert Robbins, married the local school teacher, Sarah Stevens Poinsett, from Hedding, New Jersey. My maternal grandmother, Amy, was a rugged, hard working woman who married Allen Poinsett, a farmer. Grandfather Poinsett died two years before I was born.

I was born March 27, 1917 on the family farm. My father learned carpentry, as well as farming. He built a wooden addition for us onto the back of the brick farmhouse, which was as old as Independence Hall. My memory begins when I was around three years old. A 1916 Dodge touring car and a World War I GMC Liberty Truck arrived before I remember.

On family and shopping trips my father drove the Dodge. My grandparents drove "Old Joe" and the market wagon when Daddy was busy farming. Our jaunts were short because the family was not too widely scattered. My aunts, uncles and cousins lived nearby.

---

2   1850 Census records show that John Robbins was born in New Jersey around 1790, and was living with his son Aaron and family in Bordentown, NJ

Clarence Robbins and Old Joe

During the day I spent a lot of time in Grandmother's part of the house[3]. I vividly remember her wood stove in the parlor. It was peppered with pea-sized holes through which the flames were visible. These were produced when some live dynamite was chucked in with a refill of wood! My earliest recollection of our end of the house is the combined kitchen and living room. Since it was at ground level I could go outdoors at will. At bedtime Daddy would put a blanket on the floor and I would lie on it. Then he would tuck me in, sling it over his shoulder and carry me upstairs to bed "like a sack of potatoes."

Outdoors was heaven for a small boy. Most of the house was surrounded by a fenced yard which contained grass, flowers and large shade trees. The original brick section of the house had a nice front porch which was especially useful when it rained. On one such day I exhibited a talent for entertaining children by making my baby sister laugh so hard she threw up. I was reprimanded for that. The back of the house was adjacent to the garden, grape arbor, smoke house and "backhouse."

As soon as I got big enough, I took over the farmyard, outside the fence. It contained goodies such as the wagon shed, garage for the Dodge, chicken houses and my father's work shop. Real adventure took place when I ventured into the barn and barnyard, where the horses and cows were sheltered. I never was comfortable in the stables because the horses were so big. I liked warm milk directly from the cows when the men would squirt it into my mouth at milking time. Later, I could venture down the lanes and into the fields by myself. I could even go into the meadow, and was not afraid of the cows. But there were times when my vast play yard suddenly

---

3   It was a double house for 2 families.

became off limits, and I had to dash for the safety of the nearest building. We had neighbors, directly across the creek, who owned a peripatetic bull whose frequent pleasure and business was to take over our property. When the cows were in the barn, he often came thundering right up to the back porch of the house. To this day I am afraid of bulls and have met many of them in my dreams. Grandpop could handle that gentleman with a pitchfork. And since the danger seemed so large to me, he became my first hero.

I often hitched rides on the farm machinery in the fields. The two-horse riding cultivator was an ideal place for me to sit on my father's lap and help him steer the tines along the rows of plants. I loved that machine; it taught me patience and precision.

My growing attachment to the environment beyond the farm resulted in many bawling sprints down the lane in pursuit of my father, when he left in the car without me. The lane was on Grandmother's side of the house, so it usually was her lot to run after me and bring me back. I could not understand why he would even think of leaving without me.

On Saturday evenings all the farmers and villagers did their shopping "in town." For us it was Burlington, where I still practice medicine. It was my first city, and will probably be my last as long as I can work. We piled into the Dodge with eggs and other seasonal produce which were "exchanged for some groceries and supplies. My chaperoned encounters with the merchants and other notables of the city were anticipated and enjoyed. The butchers wore straw hats and sleeves, and blood-stained white aprons. They were continually sharpening their knives tunefully on the honing rods. Paper boys chanted in the streets. Cripples sold objects along the sidewalks. Policemen directed traffic on foot and in the booth at the main intersection where the railroad crosses.

For farm supplies we went in the other direction, to Columbus. These usually were daytime jaunts, where I became acquainted with blacksmiths, mechanics, harness makers, and lumber and machinery dealers. Until recently the small town of Columbus maintained over twenty business enterprises. This town later played host to my general practice of medicine, where I treated many of the people whom I knew as a child.

Sarah Robbins and her mother Amy Poinsett with Morris outside
Amy's Hedding, NJ home.

In spite of our isolation we socialized regularly, mostly with nearby relatives. My cousins, the Lloyds, came in their horse-drawn station wagon. We still reminisce about our imaginary shooting of airplanes from the top of the old grain binder in the yard. Some mail planes and others actually did fly over the farm but, fortunately, none of them crashed from our "gunfire." By the end of the day my cousins would pass out from fatigue. Their parents had to stuff each sleeping body into convenient nooks and crannies of the wagon, to take them home.

Outdoor parties were held in the front yard. Once my bachelor uncle,[4] while chasing others around the house in a game of tag, tripped over a clothes line and broke his leg. I remember visiting him in his downstairs bedroom. This was my first encounter with orthopedics.

My father made toys for me, 1 like the wonderful two-wheeled "velocipede." It had a saddle at axle height between the tandem wheels, and my feet just touched the ground. To steer it I simply raised the front end by the handlebar and horsed it around. It ran so true that I could make ruts across the yard and imagine I was driving a locomotive. This was especially useful when there was something going on in the house that did not interest or concern me.

Even back then, farming was not all work. I remember going squirrel hunting with my father in the neighbor's woods. He did the shooting but I shared in the hunt. We also fished in the creek[5]. I used a stick and string with regular end tackle. And usually had better luck than he did. Incidental

---

4   William Briggs Robbins (1886-1968)

5   The Assiscunk Creek, a tributary of the Delaware River, bordered the farm.

daytime visits with the neighbors were pleasant, and I enjoyed the grown-ups. Sometimes they came to our establishment. Machinery fascinated me from the times when Bruce Bunting would come with his huge tractor and threshing machine to handle our grain.

Our farm was especially good for raising cantaloupes and watermelons. My first memory of calamity caused by nature was a great hail storm one summer, when our melons were ripe and ready to pick. They were completely ruined. I thought it was the end of the world!

My mother was modest and her activities on the farm were so conventional that I only remember her doing the household chores and giving me my bath by the kitchen range. Late in her life she told me that she loved farm life because it was an "institution."

My formal education began in the Jacksonville Public School, about three miles from the farm. Grandmother took me each day in the market wagon, pulled by Old Joe. Since there was no kindergarten, I was six and one-half before I started. The school building had two rooms,[6] one containing grades one to four and the other five to eight. Soon after I started, we moved to Jacksonville, a small village, to an ancient house right next *to* the school.

Farm life ended abruptly with the sale. Grandfather was retiring and Daddy wanted to continue as a carpenter[7].

I was seven or eight when we left the farm—-old enough to learn to love nature and the simpler fundamental things in life. Social life was minimal. I still do not care very much for the man-made pleasures of the city.

---

6   The school is now the Jacksonville Community Center. Sarah Robbins taught in that school.

7   The Clarence Robbins family shared a double house with Morris' grandparents Jud and Annie Robbins. Both men retired from farming at the same time, and sold the farm. Clarence built his parents a small house at 671 Delaware Avenue in Florence where they lived until they died

*The fire on the old farm, as reported in the <u>Burlington County Times</u>;
the injured firefighter was Doc's son Bill*

As I grew up, the old farm prospered as a specialty fruit and vegetable source. The cows and horses disappeared. Occasionally I would include the place in my long hikes, sampling a windfall peach or apple when available. After I became a general practitioner, I made house calls there.

For me the old farm ceased to exist a few years ago. The ground is now tilled by large-scale farmers. There is a county landfill across the creek. The house became a squatters' refuge. Early one morning it burned to the ground. The twin chimneys and corner fireplaces fell into the cellar. My son Bill, a Jacksonville fireman, was stationed with a hose by the back shed. He was directing water to tame the fire that was devouring the kitchen-living room where I hitched blanket rides from my father up to the hall bedroom. I do not want to go there anymore!

Chapter 4
THE VILLAGE

Upon moving to Jacksonville we retained the GMC and the Dodge. We rented the eighteenth-century brick portion of a house next door to the school. The owner, an elderly widower, occupied the newer wooden addition. He was a religious eccentric who taught me a lot, including grace before meals. He blamed me for everything that went wrong around the place, including the six dead mice in the well, but our friendship survived. We easily adapted to village life. I did well in school and made new friends in the area. The usual social life continued.

The Jacksonville house and mini-farm, between the store and the church.

Dad bought a new Model T Ford roadster and converted it into a pick-Up truck for his carpenter business. He sold the GMC. But just before that we took a group of young people on a hay ride in it. A storm came up while we were out, making us seek shelter under someone's open shed. When it was over, Dad cranked the engine and the truck surged forward, pinning him against the wall. I had accidentally engaged low gear!

There was an interesting mini-farm in the center of the village, between the church and the country store.[8] The place was about two acres surrounded by a wire fence to retain the chickens and various other animals. We, as a family, made several visits to the place but I did not understand why. There was a small barn, wagon shed, chicken houses and a one-acre field in the rear. Suddenly I realized that we bought the place and were preparing to move there. This was welcome news, since it resembled the old farm on a smaller scale.

We continued to raise chickens in a yard behind the barn. Since we had no other animals except a street-wise fox terrier, we opened the place up a bit and converted it into a friendly country estate with grass and flowers. Access was easier and the atmosphere became more friendly for visitors. Mother became active in the Presbyterian Church next door, and I regularly attended Sunday school and church. I became acquainted with educated people—-ministers, college students and teachers—-who were not previously accessible.

Dad maintained his farming activities in the garden, and I also developed into a gardener. I had a pet brown Bantam hen who flew up on my shoulder, rode along and talked into my ear. We used the Bantams as surrogate mothers and the Leghorns as food.

The barn became the garage for the old Dodge and the pick-up truck. The hay mow served as a storage and play room. I was agile and had learned to climb from my father, so I spent a lot of time on the roof. The "church sheds" in the next yard abutted the barn and were convenient places to play when it rained.

We had the first "stone road"[9] in the county, starting in front of our house and ending in Mount Holly, four miles distant. It was highly crowned and one-car wide. It became a highway and race track for my wooden-spoked, iron-tired express wagon with which I was expert at scooting along at high speed and great noise. I went practically everywhere with the wagon. But where it would not negotiate, I would walk, run or jump.

I made myself some stilts which were used expertly and imaginatively, usually while pretending to fly a plane. Since lumber and tools were always

---

8   Morris' great grandfather Aaron Robbins had been the postmaster and storekeeper in that store.

9   The Jacksonville-Mount Holly Road, was referred to as the "stone road" for generations.

available, I made many of my own toys and necessities. My engineering ideas often exceeded the available materials, as they do to this day.

At school, I loved my teachers. When I was promoted to the "big room" I felt rather important. There, I was a whiz at arithmetic and a show-off with the multiplication tables. At this time, Long Island, New York, was undergoing development, causing several branches of a German family to move to farms around Jacksonville. These people and their kids were solid and tough. They had what we thought were funny accents and expressions. At first, I was afraid of them but we soon became lifelong friends. I began to develop a more cosmopolitan outlook from then on.

I was skinny and could climb, jump and outrun most of the others, but was no fighter. Mother kept telling me to "turn the other cheek." To this day I am not quite sure what this means. Father also was skinny, but he was a scrapper. I was torn between his example and Mother's admonitions. As a result, I developed a diplomacy which protected me and was put to good use settling fights among my peers.

Being intellectual, I was classed with similar individuals in the community as a "sissy." Some called me "Angel Face." Deploring this image, I endeavored to change it by playing baseball and boxing, although I did not like either sport. I have always been a craftsman rather than an athlete. Gradually, the name-calling stopped.

I often managed to escape maternal surveillance by skinny-dipping in the creek with some boys, often downstream of a herd of wading cows which were trying to cool off. Occasionally some girls would discover our clothes on the bank and teasingly imprison us in the water until they felt like leaving.

While I was still going to Jacksonville School, Mother started me on violin lessons. Eventually, the Jacksonville Orchestra was formed and it ironically contained some of the people who thought I was effeminate. Although none at us were prodigies or even very good, we played at community functions at home and elsewhere for several years. Mom soon turned me over to professional violin teachers. She was the church pianist and organist for a half century.

The nationwide marble competition: Morris is front right.

In the country, where competition is not very strong, it is natural to believe you are the greatest person in the world at what you are doing. I was no exception until two humiliating experiences cured me of that misconception. I was the second-best marble player in school. The Y.M.C.A. sponsored a national marble contest. Like a fool, I picked the champion as my first opponent. In spite of my defeat I was allowed to enter at county level. There, I was eliminated on my first shot!

On another occasion we had a countywide music appreciation contest where we identified pieces and composers from records. I won locally, and went to Burlington City for the "big one." It may have been the heady atmosphere of the large auditorium full of contestants or the threat that the Jacksonville kids would beat me up if I didn't win, but something froze me into insensibility. I could not remember a single selection! This was my second great lesson –in humility. My mental block could have been stage fright, which plagued me throughout elementary school. I love classical music, but still cannot name many compositions or composers.

There were several hills in the neighborhood which became sledding ranges. I was lucky enough to own a Flexible Flyer sled, which was the best obtainable because it steered so much better than other brands. I because proficient at "belly-flopping" and was the sledding champion. In those days we hitched rides behind cars or trucks (and the school bus) by holding onto ropes tied to the vehicle. This was acknowledged to be dangerous but it was sanctioned by parents and authorities. Traffic was thinner and slower then, and nobody in our area was injured. There seemed to be more snow when I was a kid. It was, at least, deeper on the roads because the vehicles had higher road clearance, traffic was light, the roads were not plowed clean and no sand or salt was used on the hills. Thus, winter was fun.

Age 10

By the time I was ready for seventh grade, the Mount Holly school system became regionalized and we transferred there from seventh through high school. That entailed daily school bus rides which added spice to our lives. It also introduced us to home rooms, changing classes and specialized teachers. And, believe it or not, it was my first experience with modern lighting, drinking fountains and indoor rest rooms. We shared the lunch room with the high school students. Electricity came late to Jacksonville, while I was going to Mount Holly. Academically, I held my own.

Eighth grade was a high point in my early life. We used a separate four-room building for us alone and changed rooms for different subjects. We were introduced to shop, which I loved, and to gym, which I tolerated. The best part of gym was the shower, the likes of which I had never experienced. I learned later, in high school, that my nearsightedness prevented me from enjoying gym because I had to remove my glasses, which I have worn since I was nine. Eventually, the coach let me wear a catcher's type mask over my glasses. This improved my basketball by bringing the bucket into focus.

The shop was in the basement of the high school building. There were power tools that I had only seen previously at the lumber yard. I learned to use the wood lathe, band saw, table saw, router and all kinds of hand tools. We also learned some metal work such as cutting, fitting, riveting and soldering. I learned a lot from my father, but the teacher lectured and taught theory. I was with him for five years.

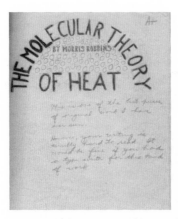

The monograph that impressed Mr. Holbein

My lady teachers were wonderful, as usual, and they seemed to take special interest in me. Most outstanding, at least to me, was my first male teacher, Francis W. Holbein. This was his second year of teaching. Science was his subject and he was born to teach. He introduced the term paper, in the form of science notebooks. I wrote the first monograph he had ever received from a student. He kept that treatise on "The Molecular Theory of Heat" the rest of his life. His extracurricular interests were the Y.M.C.A. and camping. He introduced me to the wider, more sophisticated world of overnight sleeping parties, group camping in the woods, Chinese restaurants and book stores in Camden and Philadelphia. He was an avid reader whose home library was a dream. He never married but tie loved "his boys"; We were always going places and doing interesting things with "Holbein", who claimed to be descended from the famous artist of the same name. My association with him, as his friend and physician, continued until he died.

The transfer to Mount Holly also brought me new student friends and academic competition. We competed for six years. Several of my friends were good at mechanics, music, athletics, agriculture and other things. I enjoyed visiting their homes and meeting their parents. We had an eighth-grade essay contest. My hobby and topic was the New Jersey Lenape Indians and the good stone relics which my father and I had collected over the years, especially on the farm.[10] "Holbein" had a friend who helped me with historical facts. The result was that I won first prize in the contest after we orally

---

10   Some of the Native American relics he collected have been donated to the Springfield Township Historical Society. They have been authenticated by staff of the Academy of Natural Sciences in Philadelphia.

presented our essays on the stage of the high school auditorium. I suddenly lost my stage fright and was on my way toward becoming a public speaker. At eighth grade commencement exercises I was awarded the arithmetic prize and shared the science prize with another boy.

> *"To increase our knowledge of the Delaware Indians of New Jersey, the State Museum is interested in recording all available collections of Indian Relics. Your collection has been recommended to us and therefore we would like to make a record of your pieces."*
> (Letter to Morris from the State of New Jersey Department of Conservation and Development, May 19, 1939)

Morris Robbins, Mount Holly High School student, won the applause and admiration of Mount Holly Rotarians yesterday when he was the speaker at the noon luncheon. He talked about the Indians who inhabited Burlington county and some nearby territory, telling about their habits, customs, character, and their stone implements, bows and arorws. He also presented several drawings of his own to illustrate implements. Indian study is Morris' hobby and he surely knows the subject. It was considered appropriate to have him speak right on the eve of Mount Holly's Hobby Fai-

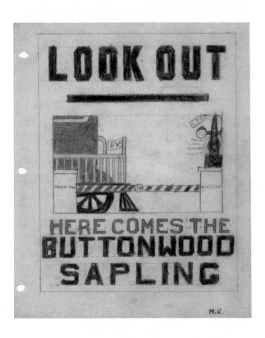

*Morris was the founder, illustrator and editor-in-chief of the school magazine,
The Buttonwood Sapling. (The school was on Buttonwood Street in Mt. Holly.)*

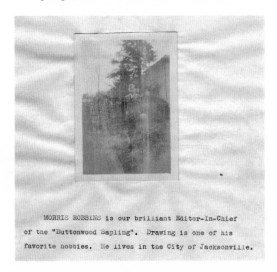

MORRIS ROBBINS is our brilliant Editor-In-Chief
of the "Buttonwood Sapling". Drawing is one of his
favorite hobbies. He lives in the City of Jacksonville.

*Among the archives donated to the Springfield Township Historical Society
is a notebook of YMCA records kept by their recording secretary/treasurer Morris
Robbins. Here is one of the pages from that notebook. Notice that the brilliant
Editor-in-Chief lives in the CITY of Jacksonville! The notebook also contains
every issue of the Buttonwood Sapling.*

Chapter 5

HIGH SCHOOL

Like most children, I looked forward to high school. The building across the street loomed so large and important. Students were permitted to choose the type of course they wanted, and I had no qualms about opting for the college preparatory curriculum. Leaving the bus, slipping past the "little kids" and crossing the street to the caverns of the big building was definitely an ego trip. Once inside, though, the enormity of it and the size and importance of the upperclassmen was again humbling. All of my academic competitors and college prep colleagues were in the same homeroom, so we became clannish. There were less than five hundred students in the whole high school.

1931; Morris, 2ⁿᵈ from right, was 14 years old; his mother Sarah is the 2ⁿᵈ from left in the back row; sister Alice stands left of Morris

Free periods, designated "study hall," were new to us. Usually we studied in the library. Being so closely associated with a real lending library containing so many books whetted my appetite for reading. My favorite topics were biography, mechanics and science. Thomas Edison was my patron saint because I pictured myself as a budding inventor[11], and he was in his prime. The medical scientists, such as Pasteur and Naguchi, fascinated me. The classics, arts and social sciences were not yet appreciated. I hated history because I could not remember the dates.

At home and in the classroom my thinness and small bone structure did not preoccupy me, since I could handle myself well in these situations. In the gym and study hall the opposite was true. The athletes were of various statures—-none were as extremely tall and beefy as they are today—-but many were more solid and heavier than I. In study hall I would stare at my thin wrists and wish I were more "normal." Little did I realize that in a very short time one of my wrists would be absent and my remaining fingers deformed.

Several of my friends suffered from physical and mental defects. I knew mongoloids (now called Down syndrome,) amputees, cerebral palsy victims, polio cripples, parkinsonians and morons. For some reason I never thought of them as freaks or pitiable creatures, but as equals with their own place in the world. I was a member of the squad in high school whose duty and privilege were to assist the non-ambulatory students in changing classes safely, and in case of fire. I was comfortable with them.

I experienced my first migraine attack as a freshman. The aura and visual symptoms scared me. This affliction is still with me in modified form. It was my first real thorn in the flesh.

I carried my violin to high school throughout the four years. Not only did I take lessons from a lovely lady in town, but I was a member of the high school orchestra. We played for assembly and other intramural activities, but never went on tour. Three of us formed an independent chamber trio of piano, violin and cello. We performed throughout the area until we graduated and went our separate ways.

---

11   As an adult, Morris invented numerous apparatuses to facilitate independence for disabled people. None of these ever were patented.

Mount Holly High School Orchestra; Morris is 4ᵗʰ from the left.

Since athletics was not my forte, I never succeeded in attaining varsity status except in track. Carrying the American flag in the color guard at football games was the closest I got. What little sports career I had, was embarrassing. I appeared for varsity basketball but was cut after the second practice. The shop teacher, who had taught me so much about tools, was the track coach. He never had time to spend with us, so we practiced on our own. Although I was a good sprinter, I was awestricken by the athletes who ran the short events, and was too shy to take them on. I picked the mile, along with two friends with whom I felt comfortable. I practiced along the roads in Jacksonville, where I put up with a lot of flak and mimicry by those who would run a few feet and announce, "I'm Morris Robbins, out for track."[12] Jogging was not the respectable social activity it is now.

In the meets I lacked the competitive killer instinct, and was too polite, letting anyone pass me who wanted to, thinking I could make it up in the end. I finished in all but the first race, but never in first or second place, and usually had to thread my way through spectators who started to filter onto the track, to cross the finish line. Only once did I receive a track award in assembly, for third place. Someone from the audience shouted, "Weren't there only three in the race?" I was good at non-varsity sports and games, such as quoits and soccer.

In spite of my public athletic debacle, I invented one-man games where the teams were imaginary and competition was intense. Hockey was played by alternately changing direction. Tennis and baseball were simulated by throwing, batting or paddling the ball against the barn, using strikes against hinges, doors, drip caps, etc. as points or fouls. Today this simulated activity

---

12   It is evident that Morris was bullied as a young man in Jacksonville and Mount Holly.

is done electronically, without providing exercise. My noisiest backyard game was "battleship", where I jumped on one of two free-rolling metal drums and bombarded the other with stones. My neighbors objected to the racket a few times. There were some interesting conventional two-man games, such as "territory" and knife throwing, at which I excelled. I still enjoy sports but, as things turned out, it is well that I have other forms of entertainment.

As class vice-president and member of the Student Council for four years I did not make history. I invented a new marking system which never got "out of committee." Academically I ranked among the top four in my class. Things did not come easily, but I was a plodder and self-disciplinarian who always did my homework. The show-off stage had disappeared, probably because the competition was greater in the big town. Physics and mathematics were my favorite subjects and the teachers were great. I could have been a decent engineer.

Socially, my life revolved around the community, church, school and Y.M.C.A. The Great Depression dominated the nation throughout my high school days. None of us was rich in earthly goods or sophisticated in our entertainment. Hiking, swimming, camping and after school labor occupied our time. I worked during summer vacations for local farmers.

Francis W. Holbein, Morris' teacher, mentor and life-long friend.

Of more personal interest and satisfaction were the few chances I had to work with my carpenter father for wages. I designed several projects which he built, and most have survived. In those days, carpenters did not use professional architects for conventional construction. Dad was an excellent carpenter. One summer we planned and built a barn, for which I earned twenty-seven dollars and fifty cents. With this I bought enough new clothing to see me through the next school year! Money came slowly and went far in the 1930s. I toyed with the idea of becoming an architect, but there was little for them to do. Some dug ditches to survive.

Mr. Holbein never let us down. He was interested in summer camping and Hi Y group activities. As we grew older, he led us into more mature experiences, both physical and mental. Two-week camping trips, canoe excursions, hobby shows, museums and the like endeared him to his former students. My first prolonged stay away from my family, many miles from home, was at his beloved Camp Wawayanda at Andover, New Jersey. I waited on the directors' table in order to spend a few weeks at camp when my parents could not afford to send me.

One of Morris' Scout handbooks

As I entered my 'teens, Mother and I became deeply involved in fundamentalist Christianity. "Billy" Sunday, the then famous baseball player-turned-evangelist, conducted a long "sawdust trail" campaign in Mount Holly, and we were "saved." I became a religious zealot for a few years' and seriously considered a theological career. Fortunately, my manual abilities and scientific interest prevented me from going overboard, but my thoughts and actions were deeply colored with spirituality. Father's practicality was strong in my hereditary pattern, and I am forever grateful for that. 1 studied the Bible daily and prayed often. Writing and "preaching" or teaching Sunday School presented no difficulty, but 1 could not buttonhole friends or strangers to attempt to convert them. (I still am not a salesman!) For a year or so I became a Lone Scout (Boy Scouts of America). At my insistence, I was appointed religious advisor to the troop. My only official activity was a "sermon on the mount" (Mt. Holly Mount), a mini-evangelistic effort. Strangely, I spoke of a man who became entangled with a hot electrical wire. Two years later the very same thing happened to me! 1 may have been a bit too religious in my adolescence but it kept me out of mischief. The fear of God is the best deterrent against evil that I can imagine.

This is the last known photograph of Morris with two hands, taken on April 5, 1935 on the Mount Holly High School Senior trip to Mount Vernon, Virginia.

I enjoyed five years of shop and mechanical drawing and, by association with my Dad and my natural talents, did well. As a senior I was appointed student maintenance carpenter, doing all the stage scenery, some minor building repairs, and making and installing a display case in the front lobby of the building. These factors have been invaluable in developing my career as a bone and joint surgeon.

Our senior class trip to Washington, D.C. was my longest journey up to that time. We took it in stride and behaved fairly well. Little incidents, such as upsetting the fire extinguisher in the hall of the hotel, riding the Senate subway and other juvenile stunts did not spoil our fun. Huey Long was haranguing the Senate and F.D.R. was out of town. I was with a group who walked all the way up the Washington Monument steps and ran down.

The traditional yearbook, "The Acorn," changed format in our hands. It had been a small paper-bound volume, but we enlarged it into a magazine-sized hard cover edition. By virtue of winning a contest to choose a new name I changed it to "The Red Oak" which it remains to this day. (Red is our color, Red Oak is our state tree, and big oaks from little [Acorns grow.) Forty-eight years later a student called me to learn the significance of the yearbook's name.

Morris Robbins—"Pop"
"He is a gentleman, because he is kind and affable to every creature."
Orchestra, 1, 2, 3, 4; Franklin Hi-Y, 1, 2, 3, 4; Glee Club, 1, 2, 3; Class Vice President, 1 2, 3; Student Board, 1, 2; Track, 2, 3, 4; Executive Council, 3; Indian Lore Club, 3; Home Room President, 3, 4; Camp Cookery Club, 4.

The Red Oak 1935

The senior essay contest was not as good as the one we had in eighth grade. My title was "The Romance of Surgery," and was not a prize winner this time. In my junior year I naively conceived the idea of building hospitals, but this evolved into the desire to become a surgeon. The ministry was not in line with my mechanical talents, but I was still very religious. The combined concept of missionary doctor was entertained for a few months because my girlfriend thought she wanted to be a missionary nurse.

I apparently shared my sweetheart with several competing swains. She was the pianist in our trio. I knew that if I went into medical training the tradition was to stay single until it was finished. That is not true today. Although deep in adolescent love, I suspected my chances with this girl were slim. She probably would not wait for me. Later circumstances also solved that problem.

Graduation day finally arrived. I shared the science prize with the same fellow as in eighth grade. I had been driving for a year, using the family car. Maryville College in Tennessee, accepted me for admission to the premedical course. My faith was strong but my financial base was thin. I expected to work my way through college and medical school. The summer had begun and my enthusiasm was high.[13]

Looking back and comparing our high school students with those of today, a few differences come to mind. There was undoubtedly some sexual activity going on but it was secret and not condoned, popularized or part of peer pressure. Most of us were innocent. Alcohol was more overt but it was usually introduced by outsiders during dances and athletic events. Prohibition was the law of the land, so procurement was difficult. Drug addiction was unheard of. pills were for sick people. Nor was discipline much of a problem, as students were fairly well-behaved. Several drop-outs returned to school and graduated. Not many of us from Mount Holly went on to college. Several attended nursing, business and trade schools, while others went directly to work. Traditionally, the girls soon married. "Women's lib" and other modern movements had not arrived. Life was definitely simpler in the early half of the twentieth century

---

13   In the 1935 <u>Red Oak</u> every single member of the graduation class, and most of the teachers and administrators signed Morris' copy.

Chapter 6

THE ACCIDENT

Mary Haines, who sat next to me in the violin section of the school orchestra for three years, was about to enter her sophomore year at Maryville College. Since the school was so far away, 1 hoped I could persuade my uncle, who was accustomed to long automobile journeys, to take Mary and me to Maryville, Tennessee. I had no experience with public transportation and my parents had never traveled so far.

On August 20, 1935 Mother and I picked Mary up at her home and started toward my uncle's farm. In a short time, we came upon a serious automobile accident involving a broken telephone or electric pole. In those days, before modern emergency squads, the law stated that you stop and give aid. I had studied medical first aid enough to be helpful. The first thing I remember is waking up in a white tent with electric bulbs shining in my face. I was injured and the victim of retrograde amnesia, which is loss of memory backwards to a certain point due to severe insults to the brain. Thus, the following account, between picking up Mary and the tent, is hearsay furnished to me by various witnesses.

A car filled with workers struck a telephone pole at an intersection just before we arrived. At that time, and for many years afterward, bare electrical wires carrying 33,000 volts crossed the intersection diagonally and ended on small wooden insulator pegs. From that point the current was fed to a transformer, on the same pole, which furnished domestic power. The accidental impact broke the pole and snapped one of the pegs, allowing one hot wire to recoil back toward the preceding pole and land along the edge of the road away from the smashed car.

The Morning Post (Camden, NJ)

When we approached the scene, I pulled around the mess and parked on
the. Left shoulder. 1 got out through the left door and walked around the
rear of my car to the accident. After the injured were on their way to the
hospital I walked around the right side of the car, intending to cross in the
front. The grass was high and wet from a previous shower. I made contact
with the bare wire in the grass, in some manner, and the wire began to
writhe and spark while barbecuing my unconscious body. A cool-headed
soldier—-God bless him—-found a dry board and clothes pole and bravely
pried me loose. (I later rewarded him for this favor.) Rumors went around
that I picked up the wire. I do not believe 1 was that stupid, and the areas of
injury to my body do not correlate with such action. The entire back half of
my body, my palms and legs below the knees were not burned. I must not
have tripped over the wire, either, but some other unknown factor caused
the contact. Maybe the wet ground and grass were charged.

I wonder how I got to the hospital since there was only one ambulance
in the area, and this was already on the way. The whole affair was etched on
the memories of that farming community, and several people told me they
saw the whole thing. Most of these individuals are gone now, as I write this
account, so I cannot verify the sequence of events.

My current next-door neighbor[14] is the nurse who had charge of the
accident ward when the casualties, including me, were brought in. She tells
me that someone brought in this body in burned clothes. She said I looked

---

14   Grace Stang McCay

dead. Without delay, I was transferred upstairs. She vividly remembers my mother keeping vigil in the hall, day after day, and refusing offers of food or drink.

> *"He means so much to me. I have been continually in prayer for him ever since he was hurt. It was nothing short of a miracle of God that Morris is here on this earth today. I commenced to pray right out loud as soon as I could talk, when some may put me in his car and took me to the hospital after they took Morris. God kept him with us, and I am sure He did it for a purpose. He has something for Morris to do. He is directing Morris' path. "The steps of a good man are ordered by the Lord" Psalm 27:33. Everything works together for good to those who love the Lord who are called according to His purpose (Romans 8:28). So , God is still on His throne, and all is well and I am content and thankful now I pray for you..."* (Letter from Sarah Robbins, August 31, 1944)

Twelve hours after the near electrocution I woke up in the previously mentioned fully enclosed white canopy illuminated by some naked electric light bulbs. There was a loin cloth and something over my left forearm and hand. Many parts of my body were encrusted in a black, aromatic, leatherlike armor. Of course, I was mystified but not quite conscious enough to be horrified. Occasionally, a pair of arms would thrust through the curtain and spray me with an atomizer. I began to realize that this was a hospital bed but I had no idea where or why. The curtains opened, after a few sprayings, and a head appeared. I recognized the person as a girl who graduated a year ahead of me and entered the Burlington County Hospital School of Nursing. I asked her why I was here and she hesitatingly told me. I had no recollection of the accident. Later, my girlfriend looked in and immediately withdrew I was told by the patient in the next bed that she fainted.

There was no day or night in the tent. The nurses told me that the spray was silver nitrate solution. It cauterized the dead and juicy burned flesh and turned it into an eschar, a natural barrier to loss of body fluids and entrance of bacteria. All of my burns were third degree.

Functionally, I was helpless. It did not take me long to realize that my left forearm was charred to the bone, which was exposed. The back of the fingers on my right hand were in a similar state. I knew an amputation of the left forearm was in order, so the announcement did not upset me anymore.

Fortunately, my right palm was intact and had sensation, but the tip of the thumb was burned. I was either too moribund or sedated to be emotional or to remember now how I felt.

My strong religious faith served me well at this point. My voice was weak, but when I said something religious, I spoke louder. I was convinced that God had saved me for a purpose and I determined to live through this experience, recover and act according to His will. I began to mentally design a prosthesis for my left arm before it was amputated.

When they finally took me out of the tent, the daily painful procedures began. To allow granulation (repair) tissue to grow over the destruction, portions of the edge of the leathery bandage were clipped away with scissors and the exposures were covered by Vaseline gauze. In the portion of the left forearm just above the wrist, where the flesh was vaporized, leaving bare bone, the median nerve was completely exposed and floating in space. When this was touched during redressing procedure, an electric shock would travel up my arm. This ability of exposed, seemingly dead, nerves to react this way is documented in medical literature.

It was not long before I was taken to the operating room for the first time. Under ether anesthesia, a guillotine amputation was done six inches below my elbow. This is a preliminary amputation of hopeless tissue by a single chop-off, without closure, to allow free drainage of any remaining dead tissue. Only the blood vessels are tied. At the first postoperative dressing change, as the bandages were carefully peeled away from the raw stump, even with morphine, I experienced the worst pain I have ever known!

Although the daily dressing change was uncomfortable, it became interesting to the point of convincing me that I still wanted to be a surgeon. Dr. Charles Schwartz, the chief surgical resident, became my idea model. He was gentle, refined, intelligent and competent, and he befriended me. He continued to nurture my budding career through my internship, several years later.

I lost so much skin that they had to use multiple grafts from my right thigh and upper part of my arms. Pinch grafts were taken from unburned areas, leaving ulcer-like punched-out holes. The pinches were placed on the raw burned surface, where they "took" in the form of tiny islands from which new skin grew peripherally. Charlie kidded me about carving my initials in my good thigh. He probably did, but so many islands were needed that the letters were obliterated. My thighs still look like a patchwork quilt. The procedures were successful.

Morris Robbins, of Jacksonville, recently returned home from the Burlington County Hospital, Mount Holly, where he underwent three skin-grafting operations on three successive Thursdays, the last operation requiring 2¾ hours in the operating room. Young Robbins was severely burned on August 20, 1935, when he went to the aid of persons injured in a collision of automobiles, and became entangled in a fallen high-tension wire of the Public Service Electric and Gas Company. As a result of the accident, it was necessary to amputate Robbins' left arm just below the elbow, and his right hand was so badly burned that he can only use the thumb and first two fingers. The young man and his father were awarded $45,000 damage by a jury on June 1, 1936, but no settlement has been made as yet, as the Public Service appealed the case.

Allentown Messenger, Oct. 29, 1936

Dr. B. Franklin Buzby, an orthopedic surgeon from Camden, took over the reconstruction process on my upper extremities. The amputation was revised to shorten the bones so the stump could be contoured and closed. It thus became less sensitive to touch. The back of my right hand was debrided (surgically cleaned up) and skin grafted, but the final result was not perfect. There was too much destruction to start with. I still cannot make a fist or bend my fingers, except at the knuckles, and the fingers are permanently curved. The middle joints within each finger, excluding the thumb, are destroyed and have become solid bone. There are no extensor tendons on the back of the same fingers and the skin is thin, delicate, insensitive and easily injured. My thumb is foreshortened (like the ape) and the nail is deformed but the joints work.

All together, over the span of two years, I was operated on, under general anesthesia, about fifteen times. The initial hospitalization was three months long. The others were frequent but shorter.

I proved to myself that necessity is the mother of invention. When I was allowed out of bed and into a wheelchair, I found that I could not propel it. We had the now old-fashion wooden chairs with wicker seats and large wheels in front. Since my right leg was the donor, and the least injured, I discovered that by crossing it over I could catch the left spokes in the heel of my shoe, and by simultaneously pushing the right hand wheel with my gauze-covered hand I could thereby propel the chair anywhere at normal speed. Of course, we had wheelchair races down the hall!

When my dressings became less bulky and I could wear proper clothing, stand and walk I was allowed in the operating room, right up to the table, to watch surgery. The only time I felt faint was when a rib was snapped from someone's chest as a procedure for treatment of tuberculosis. By this time, I was sure what I wanted to do and the right people were encouraging me.

My family and close friends were faithful in visiting me during each hospitalization. Later, I learned that my father and several others expected me to die.[15] I remember asking Mother to bring my fountain pen. She did not believe I could write with my hand bandaged. In grammar school we were drilled in the Palmer method, whereby the whole arm was used in writing, and this is the only time I ever put it to use. At home, people were very supportive, sometimes to the point of embarrassment when I wanted to do things myself.

My girlfriend entered nursing school in Newark a few days after the accident. Although we exchanged love letters for a couple of years, I never saw her again until I became an orthopedic surgeon, and I did not recognize her! At about the time I entered college, her final letter informed me that she was getting married. I was sorely disappointed and have ever since wondered if my condition was the reason.

*The Bible Student; Editor, Writer, Publisher, Artist
and Distribution Chief Morris A. Robbins*

---

15   Morris' mother Sarah later recounted that this was the first time she had ever seen her husband Clarence on his knees, praying.

During my convalescence I realized that the world had suddenly become hostile to me. Friends still treated me well but strangers acted horrified at my appearance. I had to learn to do, everything over again, in my own way, sometimes unconventionally. Fortunately, my inventive mind saved the day and I learned to handle myself. I bought an artificial arm but it would not help me in my quest to become a surgeon. Thus, my life-long research and development activities in prosthetics began. I built and experimented with my own designs and used them as well as I could. This is still going on, almost sixty years later.

Going to college was impossible for two years after my mishap because of the multiple surgical procedures and long-term bandaging. My father graciously decided to tear down the leaky old barn and build a four-car garage with a second story shop, of my own design. I taught a Sunday School class which expanded into a Y.M.C.A. club, and took the boys camping, as Mr. Holbein had done for us. My religious zeal went unabated, so I published a mimeographed monthly magazine called "The Bible Student."

After passing the road test again for driving, I bought a new Studebaker coupe which served me faithfully through my training period, courtship and marriage and into the general practice of medicine.

Those who have reviewed this manuscript insist that I reveal some of my emotions at this stage. This is difficult for several reasons. First, I am not an emotional person which, for a doctor, is an asset. Secondly, this was a long time ago and I frankly do not remember highs and lows of elation or depression. Thirdly, I was on a moderate amount of sedation which helped keep me even and maybe a bit euphoric. There was no self-pity and I planned future strategies for rehabilitation, which kept me mentally occupied. A close friend characterizes me as a fighter who has no time for despair.

I do admit to one outstanding emotion from the accident to the time I entered college. There was a high degree of self-consciousness, which is common among the handicapped. The defect could not be hidden. Gawking and talking behind the hand bothered me among strangers. I did not become a recluse, however. Later on, during and after World War II, strangers assumed I was a war casualty. One misguided individual asked me which World War I was in and I told him it was the first!

"One day (or it might have been night) I awakened and found myself in very unusual surroundings. Upon diligent inquiry I was able to learn that this strange environment was the anterior aspect of a hospital. I had experienced a major accident that walked all over anything I had ever dreamed of before. Without any warning I found myself standing at the threshold of a long hallway of suffering. I was obliged to walk the entire length alone, alone for several months, whether I liked it or not. There was no detour, so I had to do go through with it…. There were several ways, I soon observed, to undertake to outwit pain. For instance, you can throw ice water at other patients, you can fall out of bed, tear the sheets, bite your tongue, or if you are exceptionally touchy you may even slap the nurse in the face. I would not recommend that latter, however, except in cases of insanity or maltreatment. If you are interested in music you may indulge in outlandish groans. This is the method to use if you want to stop the progress of a few flying missiles of hospital furniture. Well, after weeks and months of heroic attempts at learning to behave myself even when least expected I began to learn to suffer in silence." (How I Learned to Suffer in Silence, an assignment written by Morris while at the University of Pennsylvania, October 25, 1937. He earned B+)

"Anyone who is sick or injured is bound to worry a little bit. When somebody tells you not to worry, they are trying to make you fight against nature. A person has the most courage when he is sure of himself. Like the need of the trees and plants for deep roots, so do we need something deep to carry us through hardships. This deep thing I have discovered for myself and it kept me going ever since.

"You probably have though about God while in bed because there is not much else to do but think. The closer you can get to God, Ed, the stronger you will feel. If you are right with God you will not fret or worry because you will feel Him holding you up and carrying you through." (Letter written by Morris while in college to a friend who had been terribly injured in an accident.)

Chapter 7
COLLEGE

By the summer of my twenty-first year Dr. Buzby had done all he could for me, so I applied for admission to the University of Pennsylvania. I was accepted with no difficulty in spite of my admitted handicap. Some money had become available, which eliminated the fear of being unable to pursue my ambitions. "The Bible Student" was still being published and my Sunday School class and Y.M.C.A.[16] group were flourishing. Penn, in Philadelphia, was within commuting distance in my new car. Since I was still learning to cope with my handicaps and needed my shop to continue experiments with mechanical arms, I chose to commute. This was a new experience, but I adapted rapidly to rush hour traffic and city ways. Being older than most of my classmates, I believed I could do better at home.

In 1937, Philadelphia high schools prepared students a little more thoroughly for college than small town ones. The city freshmen seemed more cultured and better educated. Because of the two-year lapse since high school graduation, I was stale. Commuting took about two hours each day, and an early start was necessary to make the eight o'clock classes. Much too often, to my embarrassment, I was a few minutes late for my first class. In spite of my best efforts, I found it hard going at first. I boned up for examinations by glancing at notes on the seat beside me while waiting for red lights and traffic jams. I eventually passed every course with fair grades, except one. My high school study habits returned and improved.

Hazing was a ritual which I did not escape. The beanie and kowtowing were tolerable. Tradition called for a ceremony in which freshmen had to kiss the toe of Ben Franklin's statue in front of Weightman Hall. The crowd was so large that, having paid my respects to Mr. Franklin, I was pushed along toward the street, managing to avoid being run over by a trolley car

---

16 Several issues of "The Bible Student" and Morris' YMCA notebook have been donated to the Springfield Township Historical Society.

by inching my way with my elbows along its side while resisting the pressure from the crowd behind me. Another close call, and so soon!

The physical education department gave me the special privilege of doing what I wanted for gym credits, without formality or competition. The regular program lasted two years and consisted of a semester in each of several sports. I could have enjoyed some of them, but it would have been rough, and I was no athlete to start with. I chose the Olympic swimming pool and the rifle range. The showers and steam room were wonderful. I enjoyed the pool and improved my swimming technique. I was best with the side stroke, with my good arm under water. I was on the rifle team, but we never met our opponents. The target sheets were collected and scored. I became expert, but not the best, using a good field rifle with a homemade rear target sight. The others had expensive target rifles. I shot by laying the barrel over my cocked left elbow or in my artificial hand. Our range was in the sub-basement of the Palestra, beneath the swimming pool. (We shot away from the tank!) Twice a week I carried the rifle on the shelf behind the car seat, in full view, with the bolt removed and placed in the glove compartment. No one challenged me or stole the rifle, even in the heart of the city. They gave me an "C" in physical education.

My most difficult freshman subject was mathematics, of all things. Premedical students were placed in a hodge-podge course that covered everything, including calculus, which I did not study in high school. The professor, in my opinion, was not top-rate, and I had difficulty. He told us that "premeds don't need much math, anyway." Chemistry was hard for me, as usual, but I managed. I was a bit slow and uncomfortable in the laboratory, but managed to complete all experiments by ingenuity.

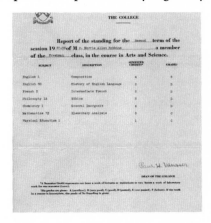

Physics was another matter. Some students hated the professor because they thought he was nasty, but I admired him and thrived. He reciprocated by sponsoring me for a student membership in The Franklin Institute. For five dollars a year I had full access to the museum, planetarium and library, and received the Journal. I attended a few meetings where research papers were presented and medals were awarded, and I enjoyed it.

The literature courses were interesting and there were some outstanding lecturers. I was exposed to writing and public speaking, and took full advantage of the opportunities. Communication is an essential part of medical practice, and I had a good chance to learn. It seemed that I spent more time preparing for French lessons than for other subjects. I became good at the language, both regular and scientific. The irony is that I never got a chance to use it after college, and have forgotten much of it. Now I wish I knew German, Italian and Spanish because many of my patients are immigrants who have difficulty with English.

Since I wanted to be a surgeon I majored in zoology and chose the curriculum leading to Major Honors. I often brought my preserved anatomical specimens home and dissected them in my shop. One basic reason for choosing this major was to train and prove myself in the most difficult laboratory procedures, such as dissection and slide preparations, both of which are manually delicate and exacting.

The subject I flunked was physical chemistry, the physical properties of the elements and compounds and the mathematics involved. The real problem was a curriculum conflict that placed me in a class of engineering students. The mathematics was brutal. I had to repeat the course but this time, being back with the premeds, I conquered it.

After completing two years of college I lost my academic disadvantage and began to forge ahead. I had a wonderful advisor, Dr. Horace Baker, who never taught me a course in his specialty of snails but who encouraged and guided me. His personal study and laboratory became a model for me, but I never was able to attain what I wanted in that regard. I still could not muster enough courage to approach certain professors in their offices when I needed help, but that obstacle disappeared by the time I reached medical school.

The Penn medical school was located on the path between the College and the Zoology Building. How I longed to enter there and get on with my medical education!

1941, age 24

In 1940 I accepted an invitation to take an auto trip across the country to Washington state with some friends who were going to visit their relatives in Spokane for the summer. The journey covered fifteen states—-the most extensive one I had ever undertaken. I learned how large and diverse America is, and did my share of the driving, without special controls, and sometimes without my prosthesis.

One of the advantages of college life is the chance to meet great and/or famous people. A highlight for me was a session with Dr. Morris Fishbein, who was the head of the American Medical Association. Some of my professors were famous in their own right. One of our students was Bob Allman who was blind but captain of the varsity wrestling team. He even made an occasional flying tackle in his matches. I met him many times when he traversed the campus alone, on foot, without a cane or dog. He crossed busy South Street that way. Joe Burke was also famous as the National Champion singles sculler. I regularly saw him practicing on the creek by his home in New Jersey, on my way to school. Now I live on the ground that was excavated from his farm to create a lake.

Premedical requirements had changed from two years of college to three, with most medical schools favoring four. I applied to the University of Virginia during my junior year and was "provisionally accepted," but was advised to finish college. Now I am glad I did because education is desirable both from the content of knowledge and knowing what to do with it.

In my senior year I spent a lot of extra time in zoology. I made some models for embryology class which survived several years. They were in the display case in the Zoology Building when I attended the Graduate School of Medicine sixteen years later. I did a year of so-called research for the physiology professor, on conduction time and its chemical alterations in frog nerves. One advantage to this was that I stayed late and missed the rush hour traffic. I don't believe much came of this project, but it was fun and instructive. In the back of my mind I was preparing for graduate work in zoology, in case I could not find a medical school that would accept me. Oddly, about two decades later my nephew, who thought he wanted to become a doctor, became a zoology professor in a university in South Carolina.[17]

At graduation I received Major Honors in Zoology, with the highest comprehensive grade in the previous ten years. Our commencement exercises were in Convention Hall, with National Poet Laureate Archibald MacLeish as our speaker. The whole university was included in the exercises.

> *"Because of a special problem, I must assure myself that the teachers with whom I work will be approachable and reasonably tolerant. The special problem of which I speak is created by an electrical burn which I suffered in 1935. My left hand was amputated above the wrist and there is some scar tissue on the dorsal surface of my right hand, which partially restricts motion, but not to the extent of disability. By sheer determination and practice, I have learned to accomplish practically everything that a normal person can do. I invent and construct artificial hands to serve the exacting purposes for which I have successfully undertaken the most difficult laboratory courses in college, in order to build self-confidence and ability to manipulate instruments and material, in order to practice techniques which, I will use in medical school. I love medicine. I plead for a chance to succeed in it or go down fighting."* (Portion of an application letter Morris wrote to Jefferson Medical College in Philadelphia, Feb. 17, 1941. He was rejected.)

Now my troubles recurred. None of the five medical schools in Philadelphia would even interview me. Penn said the student health department rejected me. I had the same experience with schools in some other cities. The only nearby school I did not apply to was the University of Maryland, because the five hundred dollar a year tuition was considered too high. I became desperate and decided to take matters into my own hands.

---

17   Dr. Lynn Morris Croshaw taught at Francis Marion University in Florence, South Carolina.

"It is my unpleasant duty to inform you...."
"...it is doubtful that we could at any time consider your application."
"...we are unable to take favorable action..."
Some of the stack of rejection letters found in Doc's files after his death.

"...your application is of such high quality that we are placing your name on our waiting list and, in case vacancies occur before the opening of the new session, we will be glad to admit you. Sincerely yours, H.E. Jordan, Department of Medicine, University of Virginia"

My cross-country buddy and I took off for Charlottesville[18] for a confrontation with the University of Virginia, to try to get them to make good on their promise. There were no interstates or turnpikes between Philadelphia and Charlottesville, and we became traffic bound in the middle of Baltimore. To my surprise, we were directly in front of the Medical School of the University of Maryland! Without hesitation I asked David[19] to park the car somewhere while I did some exploring. I boldly entered through the front door. There was no one around. I found a small elevator which was labeled, "To the Dean's office. Not for student use." Not being a student, I fiddled with the thing, but it would not open. A pleasant man came along and asked if he

---

18   See "Special man became surgeon his way" in Appendix

19   David Glenn, Morris' former pastor and traveling companion on this and on the cross-country trip

could help me. I told him I wanted to see the dean. He opened the elevator and took me to the office, where he sat down behind the desk. He told me he was the dean and was anxious to know what was on my mind. After a short, simple interview about my condition and reasons for wanting to practice medicine, and without previous application, he told me I could enter the new class in the fall, since he believed there was a place for me in medicine! We did not go on to Charlottesville. I have been forever grateful to the late H. Boyd Wylie, M. D., Professor of Chemistry and Acting Dean of the Medical School. At last the elusive prize was in my grasp.

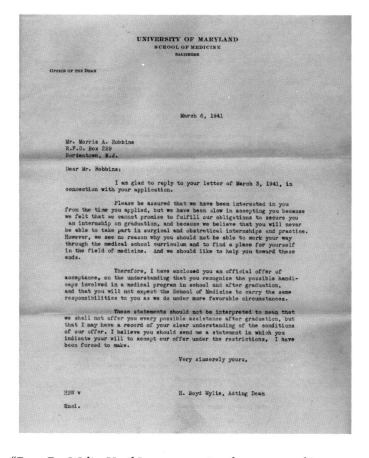

"Dear Dr. Wylie: Until I see you again, please accept this expression of gratitude for the sympathetic and practical consideration which you and the Committee have shown me. I am happy to accept your offer under the provisions which I shall state below.

I am in a position to understand the possible handicaps involved in internship and practice and I have a mature attitude toward the matter. I have no fear that you will not assist me as much as is needed and possible. However, I request the permission to undertake the entire medical school curriculum so that I may develop to the fullest extent. I refuse to be turned aside by things labelled "impossible" until I have tried. Because of the circumstances, I will shoulder a greater than usual part of the responsibility in seeking an internship, at the same time relying upon any recommendations which you can give when the time comes. "(Letter from Morris to the University of Maryland School of Medicine)

Chapter 8

MEDICAL SCHOOL:

I filled the cavernous trunk of my Studebaker and took off for Baltimore. During the summer I had obtained a room in an apartment house. Two of my Penn classmates also found rooms nearby. This was to be constant mid-city life, including parking garage, restaurants three times a day and sent-out laundry. I probably could have taken care of myself in an efficiency apartment, but there was no opportunity to look for one. I soon became tired of eating out all the time, but there was no other way. The food was strictly basic because of the constant drain on my finances and the effects of the war. For several weeks we three commuted to school in my car and ate together because our freshman schedules were identical. I was glad to have companions while gradually adapting to city living. In those days Baltimore was a rather rough town. The medical school is situated near the harbor area. Until recently it was surrounded by industry, warehouses and traffic. We were fortunate to be able to concentrate on affairs within our own buildings all day long.

I soon learned that medical school was all any student could handle. The lectures were similar to those we had in college, except for the specialization and common goal of creating physicians. Most of the laboratory classes resembled zoology and chemistry, except for frequent use of human tissues and fluids. The teachers were different compared to college, in which instructors are trained to educate, whereas graduate school faculty are only required to know the subject, and they are often difficult to follow. If college was an introduction to adulthood, medical school took us into the professional world, where we had to learn to make a living. I was thoroughly prepared for this new world, and was glad to enter it at last.

The dissecting laboratory required a short period of emotional adjustment, but it initiated us into handling human flesh. The odor of formalin penetrated our bodies, so people on the street knew we were medical students. It even seemed to flavor our food! My prostheses at this time were made of wood, wire, leather and rubber. I had little difficulty with dissection, even of the delicate nerves, and I received no special assistance. From then on, I knew I could handle my job. I found that will-power, patience and concentration can make things happen in spite of impaired manual dexterity.

The cadaver on which Morris worked was that of the late Mr. Palmer. In her twice a week letters from home, his mother Sarah often mentioned him. *"You didn't say in your letter what time you got down there Wednesday, or how you made out that evening at all. That day seemed to have slipped your mind. Mr. Palmer, I suppose, demanded so much attention."* (Letter from Sarah Robbins to Morris, Sept. 30, 1941)

I was unhappy with my housing arrangements. The kids playing in the courtyard bothered me. Human voices always distract me when trying to study. There was no place to take a short walk except for the concrete sidewalks. There were ads in the paper for rooms in the more open park-like areas of the city, and I answered one. The landlady, who was originally from New Jersey, offered me a nice room for twenty-five dollars a month and I could park my car in her yard. The Studebaker was repacked and I moved to a small brick mansion in the affluent north end, directly across the street from the famous Sherwood Gardens with their showy perennials. My room was on the second floor, with an adjacent bathroom, French doors and an open porch. There was no need to move again.

The daily ride to school was now more pleasant, there was more variety in restaurants, and more opportunity to visit neighbors and stroll in the gardens. One of my close neighbors was Glenn L. Martin,[20] of aircraft manufacturing fame. We greeted each other often on our respective ways to work.

---

20   "**Glenn Luther Martin** (January 17, 1886 – December 5, 1955) was an American aviation pioneer. He designed and built his own aircraft and was an active pilot. He founded his own aircraft company in 1912 which today through several mergers is amalgamated into the Lockheed Martin company." (Wikipedia)

Morris Robbins' draft card

Soon after we settled into the school routine all classes were mobilized because of World War II activities. All of the fellows, with two or three exceptions, were put in uniform and paid by the government. I was 4-F[21], of course, and still a civilian. The uniformed students had weekend drills and military privileges. Gas rationing was imposed and that meant fewer weekend trips home. Furthermore, the trains were over-packed and uncomfortable.

Because of the need for doctors in the service, our medical curriculum was accelerated, compressing four academic years into three calendar ones. There were very short recesses between semesters and no summer vacations. This was a tiresome grind, but it did allow me to catch up a year in my training period. Eventually I was able to start private practice at the same age as the other fellows who enlisted.

At the conclusion of the first year came the inevitable purge. We lost fifteen students, several of whom were doctors' sons. The class now numbered one hundred students, with four women. The previous surprise visit to the dean's office, a hard act to follow, was equaled in relief and thrill by the notification that I was to become a sophomore.

During his time in Baltimore, Morris received frequent letters from home, some containing money. The United States Post Office performed another important job for him – he sent his dirty laundry home to his mother. Weekly, Sarah Robbins washed and starched his scrubs and other laundry in her wringer washing machine, hung them up to dry in the yard, ironed them,

---

21   Although this card shows his status as 2-A "Deferred in support of national health, safety, or interest", later cards list Morris' status as 4-F "Rejected for military service; physical, mental, or moral reasons".

and mailed them back in a reusable mailing container. *"Hope you got your laundry on time. I insured it, like you told me. I wondered if I was going to get the juice Mon. in time to finish the ironing. I had all the white shirts left to iron Mon. A.M."* (Letter from Sarah Robbins to Morris, June 18, 1943)

Second year activities were similar to those of the first. We still were not doctors, and we never saw live patients. Our dissections progressed to internal organs, including the brain and spinal cord. We became saturated with the basic sciences of medicine, but we did not have any lessons in handling people. On the increasingly rare occasions when I could go home for a few days I began to hang around with two general practitioners, Drs. Arthur Peacock and Vernon Davis, both of whom were important to my future career. They started me on the road to the art and practice of medicine.

After two years we lost only a couple of members, and the fear of being "busted" lessened. The heavy classroom and laboratory work were finished. Things became more interesting and a bit easier to handle. With our second-half clinical education we were introduced academically to the diseases. Our basic sciences had prepared us well. The magnitude of the clinical subjects was overwhelming, and we obtained the false impression that diagnosing live patients would be easy. We did not realize that patients are not labeled and categorized, or that emotions and other mental factors interfere with the logical handling of sick people. During the vivid descriptions we would imagine we had the diseases ourselves. Whenever possible, a classroom "clinic" would be held in which patients with the disease of the day were demonstrated to us. Often, they were dramatic and experienced, exaggerating their abnormal responses. Evidently, they were paid for these demonstrations and enjoyed giving them.

Mount Holly Herald, Mar. 7, 1943;
county doctors go to war; clipping saved in Doc's files

In the third year we were still confined to the classrooms and laboratories. The hospitals were too sacred for us to enter. The surgical lessons were not as extensive as the medical ones, but we did have a laboratory where we learned techniques on anesthetized dogs. These were from the pound and would otherwise have been destroyed. Surgery on human cadavers would have taught us mechanics, but we were to keep the animals alive and recoverable. Our dog surgery was humane, like veterinary surgery. If something went wrong and the dog had to be killed, we failed. Thankfully, mine survived.

We practiced knot-tying on the furniture in our rooms. I learned to tie using my prosthesis and instruments. Suturing flesh is a different technique from tying shoes and packages and the requirements are greater.

Between the third and fourth years we had our longest vacation, the whole month of December! I applied to my "alma mater," Burlington County Hospital, for a menial clinical or laboratory job, but was assigned as a private "nurse" for a urological patient. This was still war time and qualifications were overlooked. I was not, nor will I ever be, a nurse—-an indispensable profession.

We were deprived of some of our best teachers because they had to go overseas. As a balancing factor, in our senior year and internship we were forced to pitch in as available manpower, making our education more practical than it would have been in peacetime. Thus, in some ways, we were better trained than we expected to be.

The senior year began to be fun. Now we were assigned to hospitals in the city, working both with inpatients and in the outpatient clinics. Obstetrics was emphasized, and we were exposed to a lot of it. Each of us delivered a few babies in the hospitals, under supervision. Maryland specialized in home deliveries and we actually went out to homes, on supervised assignment, to do deliveries. Although we were alone, help was as close as the telephone. Again, I was fortunate enough to stay out of trouble.

We participated in grand rounds and teaching clinics in several of the Baltimore hospitals—-except for our archrival Johns Hopkins. For me, the biggest thrill came from the surgical amphitheater, especially when we took turns assisting at surgery. My first such assignment was to hold a flashlight to illuminate the drill hole in a patient's skull during a brain operation. Because of previous experience in my home hospital the operating room did not intimidate me.

Many of the medical school faculty were part-timers who must leave their private practice for an hour or so to teach classes. Especially at Baltimore City Hospital, we would unwind with a game of touch football while awaiting the arrival of our mentor. These occasional respites were welcome.

Fortunately for us, some of our best academic surgeons were too old or otherwise unfit for the service. Dr. Charles Reid Edwards had lost a finger. He showed me that it did not handicap his operating. He had a four-finger glove custom manufactured, and he personally encouraged me to go on in surgery. Dr. Ward Grant operated on brains with one arm supported by an airplane splint. Other "normal" teachers made me feel I could make it. Dr. William R. Shipley was the Chief of the Department of Surgery. He was a formidable man who seemed unapproachable. To my surprise, near the end of my training, he called me into his office and immediately put me at ease. He somehow knew I was interested in orthopedic surgery, and he told me to go ahead with my plans! I was advised to be careful of infections to protect my remaining anatomy. Antibiotics were just being introduced at this time. After this momentous interview I figured that nothing would stop me. Seniors volunteered in the Emergency Room, where I learned to suture living flesh, especially faces. The local populace had a penchant for razor slashing, especially on Saturday nights.

I will never forget the gynecological clinic, where we learned to do pelvic examinations. As usual, I had to develop a special technique. We had a patient who had a bicornuate (double) uterus and a double vagina, one side of which did not enter the womb. Someone had told her that she had two openings inside, "one for business and one for pleasure." About once a year she would come back and request reexamination because she forgot which side was which!

The University and other local hospital internships usually went to favored students. Rather than applying for one of these, I aimed for the largest hospital in southern New Jersey—-Cooper, in Camden, near my home. Dr. Buzby was Chief of Orthopedic Surgery there, so I hoped he could do something for me.

One weekend, my father picked me up at the train station in Philadelphia. I asked him to stop at Dr. Buzby's office in Camden. Repeating the brazen surprise attack, I barged into the waiting room and asked the receptionist to let me see the doctor. She raised a fuss because I did not have an appointment, but I asked her to please tell her, boss that "Doctor" Robbins was here. I could hear him shout, "Doctor Robbins?" He came flying out to the waiting room, put his arms around me and gave me a lecture for not telling him I was in medical school. I told h1m I wanted an internship at Cooper in October. He called Cooper, dropped everything, and literally dragged me over to the hospital. There was an immediate administrative conference, and within an hour I was appointed as incoming rotating intern, number thirteen on the already full list of twelve. This is the last time I tried that tactic.

Now I could coast along toward graduation, knowing that the next step was accounted for. This was a good hospital where I might continue to practice after my internship was completed. Our commencement speaker was Dr. Norman T. Kirk, Maryland alumnus, orthopedic surgeon and Surgeon-General of the United States. When my turn came to meet him and receive the diploma he said, in a low voice, "Take it with your prosthesis." He surprised me so that I momentarily froze, then took the document conventionally, with my right hand. He complimented me privately and I started to leave the stage. The entire graduating class arose from their seats, threw their hats into the air and shouted, "Hoorah, Robbins!" I packed the Studebaker for the last time and came home, in time to start my internship in a few days. I was Morris A. Robbins, M. D., and already licensed to practice in Maryland pending completion of internship in any state.

"When he went up to get his diploma was another big moment. The big high man of the class with the highest mark was applauded all the way to his seat. And when it came to Morris, they did the same thing for him" (letter from Sarah Robbins to Betty Sutton, Oct. 6, 1944)

The President, The Regents and the Faculties

of the

School of Medicine and the School of Nursing

of the

University of Maryland

request the honor of your presence

at the

Graduation Exercises

Friday evening, September twenty-ninth

at eight o'clock

The Lyric

Baltimore

Chapter 9

INTERNSHIP

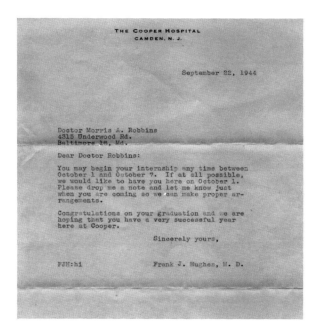

My long-anticipated internship began on October I, 1944. The program had been shortened to nine months from the original twelve because of the accelerated wartime training. Being a civilian, I was uncertain whether or not I could get away with nine months, so I volunteered to stay a whole year. We received the enormous sum of fifteen dollars a month, plus room and board, and part of that was withheld for income tax. The relief of having regular meals three times a day in the same dining room compensated for the lack of income. Another bonus was regular trips home every other evening, except for weekend duty, and every other weekend off. Cooper was less than twenty-five miles from home, so there was enough gas for this distance. There was no available public transportation from Jacksonville. My commuting was similar to college, but shorter.

I immediately began the routine of interrupted sleep which continued through many years of practice. Although I had become accustomed to studying long into the night in school, this was both physically and mentally draining.

> *"'Tis Sunday night again, and I have had the weekend off, and I'm closing it by my usual, and favorite, activity, namely this. To write more often would indeed be much better, but it takes a lot of time for me to write a letter, and it takes still more time to meet the multitudinous demands of my patients. What is more, I cannot sit down alone for more than 10 to 15 minutes at a time when I am on duty, except in the very dead of night, so you can see that writing is next to being impossible except when I have a weekend. When I get a weekday night off, I'm too tired to do anything but sleep, as I am then relatively undisturbed."* (Letter from Morris to fiancé Betty Sutton, Nov. 19, 1944)

The war was still on, so we had to do more practical things and take on more responsibility than was usual for interns. The attending doctors were either in the service or overworked at home, and the latter had to delegate many of their duties to us. We also received unusual experience with out-patients, since we had to man the clinics, which were heavily utilized. Most of my fellow interns were from Philadelphia medical schools and were local men who intended to practice in the area after they finished their service requirements. As interns, we were closer and more dependent upon each other than were medical students. Some of the group were sons of physicians and surgeons who were well-known in the Camden area and on the staff at Cooper. This would be a distinct advantage to me if I later practiced in the area. For several months I had no idea what I would do next, but at least I was finally established in the medical profession.

A rotating internship consisted of four to eight weeks in all departments of the hospital. It was mandatory before entering independent practice in the United States. The idea was to turn out well-rounded doctors regardless of future specialization. By chance, I started in the nonsurgical field, which gave me an opportunity to develop my own techniques without the pressure of operative surgery. I gained experience in history taking, physical examination, diagnosis and treatment before learning to operate. Medicine and pediatrics were my most interesting nonsurgical Subjects. As a result of my practiced concentration and over-compensation, I became expert with the needle. In fact, I often was called to do difficult intravenous procedures for my colleagues, and I actually became the needle expert of the group.

Miss Elizabeth Sutton,
Radford School for Girls,
Austin Terrace,
El Paso, Texas

"Don't become too alarmed at the "engraved" envelop and letter head. These, my dear, are hand made by one of my patients who is an engraver. This beautiful work is just an example of what you and I are to expect in the future, for patients often pay their doctors by examples or samples of their work, whether they be farmers, craftsmen, or professional people. This particular fellow does beautiful work, but unfortunately, he has a fatal disease which will not spare him for long. It's just one of the tragedies of life that medical people must stand by and watch, helplessly in regards to the final outcome. To add to the tragedy, the surgeon who did so much to mend my body after my accident is dying of the same disease, and is doing it in Cooper Hospital." "(Letter from Morris to fiancé Betty Sutton, Oct. 16, 1944)

For some time, I had heard rumors that Dr. Buzby had leukemia. Although he looked thin when I surprised him in his office, I did not realize how sick he really was. A few months into my internship he was admitted in critical condition. I visited and cared for him daily. Toward the end, he would not let any doctor in his room except me. When he died his family notified me first. I not only lost a friend and benefactor, but also my secret hope of going into orthopedic surgery with him.[22]

In the '40s it was easy for people to get admitted to a hospital and stay there awhile. A high percentage of our inpatients were on welfare, and it was a convenient place for them to be when they could not care for themselves.

22   Dr. Benjamin F. Buzby died of leukemia at age 53 in 1944.

As a result, we interns treated a wide variety of real and imagined illness. We also learned for the first time how to handle people. Each ward accommodated thirty or more patients. Our outlook was broadened by sharing the care of semiprivate and private patients.

With such a diversity of population, things occasionally got out of hand. I was assigned to a patient who occupied a private room in an isolated part of the hospital. The room was always full of visitors, male and female, as was the hallway outside. I do not recall his diagnosis, but he needed intravenous therapy and frequent examination. His visitors kept asking questions and watching everything I did. The man suddenly died! Without realizing it, I was trapped by his bedside, and the atmosphere became hostile. The nurses must have spread the alarm because our largest intern, Dr. John Pulliam, and some other people burst into the room and rescued me. Only then did I learn my patient was a local gangster and his visitors were members of the mob. They had threatened to kill me! John, a local urologist, and I occasionally reminisce about this episode.

Accident ward duty was a highlight of my internship and a cram course for the next stage of my career. Many patients were the same type as in Baltimore, so I perfected my cosmetic surgery. We had medical decisions to make and treatments to give, often before we were able to contact our superiors. Camden, an industrial city, guaranteed us a constant supply of trauma cases. We set fractures and repaired soft tissues daily. I spent the whole year on this service, in rotation and coverage. We became acquainted with the policemen who brought patients in.

One of our duties was to sober up drunks long enough for them to identify themselves, so the police could take them home. We injected a heart stimulant intravenously which has an immediate, but transient, effect on muddled brains. This drug was later pronounced too dangerous, even for heart patients, but it was a godsend to the police officers at the time.

Because of a drowning in a city swimming pool a nurse and I were rushed to the scene in a patrol car. Despite the lights and siren, we had a near collision. Unfortunately, the victim could not be resuscitated.

There was one unforgettable lesson I learned in the accident ward. A man came in with mangled fingers. I carefully set the fractures and neatly sutured the wounds. He was referred to Dr. Robert Gamon, one of my favorite general surgeons. The next day Dr. Gamon congratulated me on the fine suturing job, but told me he took every suture out! He reminded me that crush wounds swell and the resistance of the sutures could cause 'gangrene. Later on, my patients were skeptical when I heeded this advice, even after I told them why. One of the most difficult medical decisions is to refrain from doing certain things. This is why patients and lawyers should not challenge the doctor in judgmental matters.

Soon after I began accident ward duty some policemen were standing nearby watching me administer to their patient. One of the officers said, "I heard there was one here." I presumed he was referring to the one-armed intern. They apparently accepted me, never gave me any trouble, and let me do my job.

Except for the odd hours, obstetrics always fascinated me. Cooper had a special building devoted to maternity, and the service was very active. There were two obstetrical residents who, with the help of the interns, handled all the ward cases. We were also allowed to deliver babies, with or without supervision. We assisted private obstetricians and often delivered for them if they were late. There was a lounge and separate sleeping quarters for those of us on duty.

I had no special difficulty with deliveries, partly because I used my abdomen to hold the baby back while extricating it with my right hand. By the combined use of my right hand and cradling with my prosthesis, I handled the transfer of the baby, clamping and cutting the cord, starting respiration and delivering the infant to the bassinet. I worried as much about dropping the baby as anyone else, but was spared that disaster.

I learned to respect the problems of gynecology and the complications of obstetrics. I even had the dubious honor of being first assistant to Dr. Hammel P. Shipps when he removed my mother's uterus—-my first home! It took some nerve on my part, but he asked me to help and it was my assignment. Orthopedics was my primary interest, but I appreciated the well-rounded training.

Speaking of gynecology reminds me of the young man in Navy uniform who waited in the intern quarters for a cute little assistant dietician. He was Dr. Alan Schaeffer, who became an obstetrician/gynecologist, married Nancy Cox, worked with Dr. Shipps and moved to Delanco. About a decade later I moved to Delanco and became his neighbor, worked in his hospital, and recently hired his office nurse after he retired from practice

Our pediatric department was huge and active. The ward was supervised by a tough nurse who tolerated no nonsense, but she knew her business. To those who swallowed their pride and cooperated she was a friend and excellent teacher. She taught me more pediatrics than the doctors did. She even called me when she wanted some special procedure done.

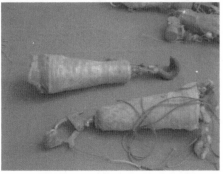

Early protheses made by Doc

While still in medical school I bought a split-hook prosthesis and attached it to one of my sockets. This is an effective and still standard end piece but, being cold and hard, it scares children. I used it almost exclusively during my internship. It aided in handling syringes, needles, vials, tongue blades, sutures and bandages. With it I could tie my own cap and mask and put on rubber gloves. However, it did not dampen my interest in improving the mechanical arm, in which I later succeeded to the point where I seldom use the hook anymore.

Assignments to the surgical services came in due time. I did everything an intern was supposed to do, both in the operating room and the wards. I used my prosthesis to hold the scrub brush for my right arm. With the brush in my right hand I scrubbed the prosthesis, which was waterproof and the mechanism was completely exposed to the solution. At that time the surgical scrub was tincture of green soap followed by a dip in dilute carbolic acid and further neutralized and rinsed with alcohol. This was a good lubricant for my hook. I gowned and gloved conventionally, filling two fingers of the left glove with the prongs of the hook and tucking in the empty fingers. My relationship with the attending surgeons was good, and they did not hesitate to use me as first or second assistant and for follow up wound care. I reduced my share of fractures under local or general anesthesia and applied casts. Supervision was not always available because the war was still on.

After nine months my intern class finished and went into the Service. The administrator let me stay another three months as intern~at-large. This allowed me to plunge deeply into orthopedics. Dr. Oswald Carlander was the only orthopedist on the staff who remained a civilian, and he was extremely busy. I took over the orthopedic clinic, often without him. For difficult decisions and procedures, I would have the patients come back to the accident ward on Saturday mornings and he would help me. Two afternoons a week I went to his office as an extern and learned to handle an office practice.

COLUMBUS PHYSICIAN TO TAKE PHILA. POST

Columbus, Aug. 15.—Dr. Arthur B. Peacock will leave his practice of medicine here Oct. 1 to accept a staff appointment at Pennsylvania hospital, Philadelphia. He and his family are moving to Moorestown. During the past 12 years in which he practiced here he was on the staff of the Burlington County hospital.

Dr. Morris Robbins, of Cooper hospital, Camden, will succeed Dr. Peacock here.

Courier-Post, Aug 15, 1945

Before my year was finished, Dr. Peacock came to see me at the hospital. He asked about my plans for the future. Since we were still at war with Japan, I told him I wanted to go into general practice in a small town, like Columbus, for a while. He told me he was leaving Columbus and offered me his property and practice! This was a surprise attack, in reverse, and I immediately accepted.

This startling development called for some quick planning. I had to borrow money to buy the property, but the practice was mine for the taking. At some point during medical school I developed a love for Elizabeth Sutton, a life-long friend. She was working in El Paso, Texas as a dietician in a girls' school[23]. While she was there, we began writing to each other and exchanging pictures. At about the time I graduated she left Texas and came back home to work for Drexel University. In my condition, I had no idea what women thought of me in terms of matrimony. Our face-to-face courtship spanned my intern year, when I could get home for an evening or weekend. I don't

---

23   Radford School for Girls, El Paso, Texas

remember our going anywhere or doing anything together, because of lack of time. I felt that Dr. Peacock's legacy was overwhelming and demanding, and I needed a wife to help me handle it. I mustered my courage and proposed. When she accepted, I could hardly believe it!

COLUMBUS.

There was a very pretty wedding on Saturday afternoon, at 5 o'clock, in the Providence Presbyterian Church of Bustleton, when Miss Elizabeth Sutton, daughter of Mr. and Mrs. John M. Sutton, of Mystic Valley Farm, Bordentown, was married to Dr. Morris A. Robbins, son of Mr. and Mrs. Clarence Robbins, also of Bordentown. The ceremony was performed by the Rev. Charles F. VanHorn, pastor of the First Presbyterian Church of South Amboy. The bride was given in marriage by her father. Her sister, Miss Anne Sutton, was her only attendant. Robert Croshaw, of Mount Holly, acted as best man, and the ushers were Dr. David Brewer, of Woodbury, and Fred Parkes, of Bordentown.

Allentown Messenger, Sept 27, 1945

"I received a valuable piece of literature in the mail one day this week. It was my Maryland license to practice Medicine and Surgery. A welcome contribution to my worldly possessions. Now I will be able to practice in any one of 44 states if I have the price to pay for the reciprocation fee, without further examination. I believe I am the only intern on the Cooper Staff with a license."
(Morris' letter to fiancé Betty Sutton, Feb. 5, 1945)

Cooper gave me a few days grace at the end of my contract, when Betty and I were married in her home church. My best man was one of my fellow interns. Since I already had been granted a medical license in Maryland, I could reciprocate with New Jersey for a fee of one hundred dollars. Betty and I spent a weekend honeymoon in Asbury Park, New Jersey, and then moved into Dr. Peacock's home and office in Columbus.

Although the public did not know it, my license had not arrived by the time we moved in. I had to turn away several people. The license was dated October 1, 1945.

Chapter 10
GENERAL PRACTICE

The house and office at 39 West Main Street, Columbus, New Jersey, with the Studebaker parked out front. The office entrance is on the right side of the picture.

I replaced Dr. Peacock's shingle with my own and parked the Studebaker in the same spot where his Lincoln Zephyr had stood, indicating I was available. He left me his office furniture and medical supplies, so there was hardly a ripple in the practice—-except for the greenhorn at the helm. In my circumstances, familiarity with the community was an asset. Had I gone to a strange place, the amputation might have been too much for people to accept. The doctor left his records and prepared his patients for transfer to me, including several almost due maternity cases, some to be delivered at home. I changed the office hour schedule slightly to allow me to continue helping Dr. Carlander on his mornings in the operating room and on Friday afternoons in the Orthopedic Clinic.

People appeared so fast in the first week—-as many as twenty-four a day—-that it almost equaled a day in the accident ward at Cooper. I realized that supply and demand was partly responsible, since several of the local doctors were still in the service. At least half of the patients demanded house calls. This was actually a welcome relief from the years-long confinement at school, commuting against the clock, and internship. I learned the countryside like a taxi driver, and traveled a lot at night. One great advantage of house calls in general practice is knowledge of the background and lifestyle of the patient. In 1945, Columbus was the center of a contiguous farming community. My territory included three townships and several small towns, so I was constantly driving and even retracing my steps the same day. Except during office hours, my poor eight-year-old Studebaker hardly had time to cool down.

> Ronald Carty, son of Mr. and Mrs. Lloyd Carty, fell downstairs at his home on Wednesday, March 30, hitting his head against the newelpost with such force that a splinter the size of a little finger was broken off the hardwood post. He was taken to Dr. Morris Robbins, of Columbus, where two stitches were required to close a gash above one ear. Just three weeks before, Ronald was accidentlly hit by a baseball bat at recess at Columbus School, and Dr. Robbins took one stitch to close a cut in his forehead.

> cing after being confined to bed for a week with bronchitis, under the care of Dr. Morris Robbins. Callers included Mrs. Alice E. Potts, of Hedding; Mrs. George Parker, of Jacksonville; Mrs. Russell Roberts and Miss Jeanette Roberts, of Kinkora; Mrs. Joshua A. Coulter, Mrs. Morris Robbins. Mrs. Joseph Schulze and Rev. William Shea, of Columbus.

> Charles Wainwright injured the little finger of his left hand while operating a tractor on the farm of his father, Raymond Wainwright, on Friday. He was treated at the office of Dr. Morris Robbins, of Columbus, four stitches being required to close the wound.

In the small country town of Columbus, every detail of daily life was reported in the local newspaper. This was before any aspect of a Privacy Act. Dr. Robbins' name appeared in almost every issue of the Allentown Messenger.

The headiness of my new importance embarrassed me several times in the first few weeks. A case in point was my first home delivery, which took place in Mount Holly, the county seat. My bag was properly supplied and I knew how to deliver babies. I took my intern clothes, so I could change into them and present a clean and professional appearance. To my chagrin, I could not get the trousers closed around my suddenly expanding belly! My dietician wife had fed me so well that I gained weight quickly and was no longer the bean pole I had always been.

The war stopped, but peacetime economy was hardly in gear. The Studebaker began to break down on emergency calls, and I resorted to borrowing cars. There was a dealer in town who received his first post-war Ford sedan. It was promised to a local farmer, but he decided to sell it to me for around eleven hundred dollars cash. I have been a "Ford man" ever since.

Things were going well, but I knew that sooner or later something would happen to bring me back to reality. A flu epidemic hit town about four months after I arrived. It was especially hard on old people, and Columbus was noted for its elderly population. I lost five people in less than a month, and some lived across the street from me. One was the mother of the man who later became my fishing buddy. I was scared and discouraged, but the community supported me and did not seem to hold me to blame. If that happened today, I would probably be sued and run out of town. This was the worst experience I ever had with multiple consecutive deaths.

The Internal Revenue Service jumped me three months after I started practice. The auditor wanted to know where the rest of my money was. I reminded him that I had just begun, and had no money. After more interviews and paper shuffling, he finally left me alone.

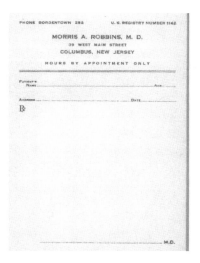

After this dual baptism of fire, things settled down toward Spring. There seemed to be no doubt that I was entrenched, and my practice flourished. I inherited the two-dollar office visit, three-dollar house call and twenty-five-dollar delivery. A steady, but modest, income was a new experience for me. Thanks to my humble background and Betty's frugality, we did not spend foolishly, but there was no way to accumulate capital.

The Columbus practice had an unusual feature which increased the overhead as compared to my colleagues. A previous doctor had a drug store on the corner. After he died, no one bought his business. Therefore, Dr. Peacock, who was not a pharmacist, saw fit to dispense his own drugs. When I took over, the office contained a wide variety of medicines. A lot of these were "ethical," but most were repackaged products from small direct-selling companies, obtained through traveling salesmen. After the war, the "detail men" were in their glory. They overwhelmed me, and my sales resistance was not very strong. Patients expected me to dispense, as Dr. Peacock did. Since there was no drugstore within miles, I felt obligated to continue supplying medicine. There was a satisfying completeness to my practice because it was so self-contained. I had been taught that when a person consults a doctor, he expects to take some medicine home. I never broke even on the drug bill, and the patients got off cheaply. If a drugstore had opened in town, I would have given up the up dispensing. The "pill mill" lasted throughout my general practice. In fact, after a few years I had to remodel the storage facilities to hold the jars and jugs full of pretty pills, capsules and liquids. The place smelled like a pharmacy.

At around 11 or 12 years of age, I began to lose weight and was often too tired to even go to school. Dr. Peacock was unable to make any diagnosis, nor did he make any referrals. But when Dr. Robbins came to town, Mother took me to him and he immediately recognized the problem and referred me to Cooper Hospital where the cardiologist diagnosed Rheumatic Fever. (This was prior to penicillin.) In those days the recommended treatment for this illness was complete bed rest for 3 months, followed by 3 more months of limited physical activity. Your Dad came out to our home frequently and was about the only visitor I had as many of the family and friends wrongly thought I was contagious. (Of course, the strep that caused the R.F. was long gone by then but they didn't understand that!) My parents were very grateful to this young doctor and he and your Mom and my parents developed a warm friendship through the years, but this occasion was the beginning of our affectionate relationship with the Columbus doctor who became beloved by so many. (Jean Bryan McClure, former patient)

In my general practice days minor surgery was routinely done in the doctor's office if general anesthesia was not required. Litigation and insurance companies later discouraged office surgery, but now there is pressure to resume it to reduce cost. They should have left us alone in the first place! We knew how to keep costs under control, but were not given credit for it. Not only was I inclined toward surgery, but the Columbus area needed a lot of it. Someone was always getting cut and needing suturing, the removal of dirty and hopelessly injured tissue, or excision of lumps. I had my own autoclave, instruments and drapes, so sterility was no problem. By tying with instruments and using the "no touch" technique, I avoided contamination. The handles were laid outboard of the instrument tray so the working end of the forceps, scissors and needle holders remained sterile. The tissues were tested and manipulated with forceps rather than the fingers. As a safety precaution, sulfanilamide powder was sprinkled over the wound, like salt. Sulfas were in vogue, and were very effective. They were bacteriostatic, rather than antibiotic, meaning that bacteria could not reproduce. Antibiotics actually kill the present colony of bacteria.

One surgical technique I cannot handle is to pick up and manipulate tissue with the common thumb forceps in my left hand while operating with the other. My special technique is to clamp a hemostat onto the edge of the tissue and hold and move it with the instrument held in the left artificial hand. There has been no problem in this regard.

Most office surgery was routine. It could be amusing, critical or exasperating. The ever-present danger of having a patient faint was usually counteracted by having him lie down. Among farmers it was not manly to consider the possibility of so feminine a thing happening. They wanted to sit up and watch the procedure. One of my favorite farmers was six feet tall and two hundred thirty pounds. He came in with a large splinter embedded in his thigh. I wanted him to lie down, but he insisted on sitting upright on the table with his legs dangling over the side. I sat on a stool with my eyes level with his thigh. After injecting a local anesthetic, I put on my binocular magnifiers, approached the focal distance of eight inches, and proceeded to carefully cut down to the wood. Suddenly, the wound went out of focus and the table began to tilt. The patient had fainted! He landed on my shoulder and slid to the floor. After breaking his fall, I completed the job on the floor. He was sheepish and I was muscle strained.

The critical cases involved bleeding. People came in with all kinds of tourniquets and pressure dressings, usually saturated with blood. Laymen usually could not assist because many passed out at the sight of blood. The dressings had to be carefully peeled away while searching for the bleeding points to be clamped with hemostats. Then the wound had to be cleaned and the bloody material taken out of range. I had to tie, unclamp and repair the damage alone, unless the patient was thoughtful enough to get hurt when my office nurse was with me.

One Sunday morning a farmer came in to have a sebaceous cyst removed from his back, close to his spine. I had developed a technique of releasing these cysts from the skin by cutting around the original pore like a collar. After evacuating the cheesy contents, I would twist the wall of the cyst out, with minimal bleeding. Sulfa powder stopped whatever oozing there was. But this man's cyst was like an iceberg. The noticeable lump was similar to the pointed end of a pear, and the larger mass was spread out in the subcutaneous fat to an unexpected degree. I had no assistance, and the dissection became deeper and wider. There was no chance to twist the devilish thing out. I ended up with the spine exposed over an area the size of a silver dollar. I kept calm and sutured the wound, but was glad when it was over, as an elective office procedure. Healing was uneventful.

Betty had an uncle who flew an open cockpit plane and wore aviator's cap and goggles. He would fly from his home in Cleveland to her father's farm every Fourth of July. This was a community tradition where his relatives and old friends gathered to visit him. His last flight was no different from the rest, until he took off for Cleveland. He left the farm and landed at a small airport a few miles away, to gas up. On takeoff his engine died as soon as he was air-borne. Rather than endangering traffic on the busy highway near the hangar, he pancaked between buildings. He had forgotten to open the tank valves after refueling, and the engine drained the carburetor. They brought him to my office, where I spent several hours carefully removing shards of glass from his face and repairing multiple lacerations. He was seventy years old, and usually flew alone. When I finished with him, he announced that from now on he was going to wear plastic goggles!

In order for me to handle the inherited and acquired hospital deliveries, Dr. Peacock made sure I received a staff appointment at Burlington County Hospital, where I had previously been a patient. This assignment included medicine, minor surgery and closed reduction of fractures under general anesthesia. The hospital was ten miles from my office. This was a major factor in making the office the stopping-off place and treatment center for local injuries and medical emergencies. Emergency squads were just being organized and were not very efficient as yet.

Dr. Carlander took care of me at Cooper by having me appointed Assistant Orthopedist to Outpatients, meaning I could officially work in the orthopedic clinic. I could not use Cooper for anything else, but it was too far away to be practical for my inpatients, anyway.

The bulk of general practice was routine colds, flu, gall bladder attacks, heart trouble, children's' shots, female problems, nervousness, sprains, fractures, scrapes, bruises, intestinal disorders, vomiting, diarrhea, indigestion, insomnia, nosebleeds, bleeding gums after the dentist had left for a weekend at the shore, weight reduction, hypertension, headaches, dizziness" weakness, ear wax, dirt in the eye, boils, rashes, hives, psychoses, and what have you. These problems demanded attention and kept food on the table, but my primary interests were obstetrics and orthopedics. I tolerated the rest, but maintained a desire to break away from general practice.

I worked in both Burlington County and Cooper clinics for around twenty years—-Tuesday afternoons at Mount Holly and Friday afternoons in Camden. In addition, I assisted Dr. Carlander and also Dr. Davis, after he returned from the Army as an orthopedic surgeon, on their operating mornings at both hospitals. Private practice suffered somewhat, but my orthopedic interests and abilities grew. I kept up this operating routine until I left for a residency in orthopedic surgery.

In these days of paramedics, coronary care units, monitors, open heart surgery and bypasses, it is difficult to imagine that, when I was in Columbus, heart attacks were treated at home. Coronaries resembled gall bladder attacks and other forms of indigestion so much that the diagnosis often was not certain unless the patient died. In order to obtain an electro-cardiogram, I had to call in a consultant with his portable instrument. Our community hospitals did not admit patients with heart problems.

My Ford dealer came home from a banquet and developed severe chest and epigastric pain a few hours later. During the night I diagnosed gall bladder attack and treated him accordingly. A day or two later Dr. Peacock, who was now an internist, brought his E.K.G. and diagnosed coronary occlusion. He helped me care for this man, at home. Things seemed to be going along well for two weeks, when my patient and friend died. He was an example of what happens in coronary occlusion. The patient either dies immediately from cardiac arrest, ten to fourteen days later from rupture of the heart muscle (as the Ford dealer did), or recovers. Today, the same thing happens, in spite of high technology. If you make it to the hospital or have your attack while in the hospital, your chances of resuscitation are better. We believe new drugs and surgery prevent or postpone fatal heart attacks. It is well that hospitals have changed their admission policies.

The same was true for patients who suffered strokes. They also stayed home. The Ford dealer's secretary lost her mother from a stroke. I could not take her to the hospital, but did my best for her in her home. If these patients recovered, we tried to restore function without the fancy and expensive modern rehabilitation centers. I believe cardiac patients receive more benefit from today's techniques than stroke patients do because of the pathology and anatomical involvement. Damaged brains and spinal cords still cannot be repaired and restored, but hearts may be persuaded to keep on pumping.

There were a few diseases I knew too little about. Diabetes baffled me and I did not hesitate to refer these patients to someone else. Blood and urine sugars could be quickly checked in the office, but most diabetic crises occurred at home or elsewhere, far from the office. Strange as it may seem, the visible skin diseases all looked alike to me. The itches and blisters could be controlled, but the more exotic rashes and patches required the services of a dermatologist.

Urological problems, such as stones and prostatic obstruction, were easy as far as catheterization and relief of pain were concerned, but definitive care was obtained at Burlington County's excellent facilities. Dr. Lloyd B. Greene divided his time between Mount Holly and Philadelphia. He not only was an excellent urologist, but an outstanding man and friend of the general practitioner.

One day I bought a small X-ray machine, especially for limb fractures. In the public's view, I became a better doctor immediately because I could find what the trouble really was. Without restraint, I could have capitalized on this. People came directly to my office when they thought they had broken a bone. I could examine, X-ray and set the bones within the first golden hour when the area was numb and still flexible, often without local anesthesia. Today, that opportunity is lost because the patient awaits the ambulance, goes to the emergency ward of a hospital, is subjected to all sorts of red tape, waits for his turn in the X-ray room and for the radiologist to read the films, then waits still more until the orthopedic surgeon arrives sometime later. Then, if the fracture cannot be reduced under local anesthesia, there is a further wait until the anesthetist and the operating room can be mobilized. Often, the patient has just eaten, and general anesthesia must be postponed for six or more hours. The golden hour has expired. The fracture has become stiff, painful and swollen, making reduction more difficult even with the patient asleep. In return for expert specialist's care, the patient may pay in increased risk and complications. All progress is not necessarily improvement.

I enjoyed treating fractures, both in office and hospital. Yet, in spite of the fact that I had assisted the orthopedists with so many open reductions where it was necessary to expose the bone, manipulate it and secure it with metal, I was not allowed to do my own cases in the operating room. These fractures were referred to the orthopedic surgeon and I usually assisted him, gratis. It still was my intention to give up the nosebleeds and skin rashes for the privilege of expanding my bone surgery when I could make the move.

Medical practice involves sudden or slow death in young or old. As shocking as my early experience with the elderly flu victims was, I learned to take it in stride, but did not like to deal with it. It was one thing to have old people expire from the complications of age or disease, but quite another when middle-aged people or children died. In the hospital, autopsies were performed and the patient contributed to general and personal medical knowledge. Families now are more resistant to post-mortem examinations. They not only are helping decrease the personal concern of the doctors, but are cheating themselves in as far as knowledge of hereditary traits and possible insurance benefits are concerned. The pathologist does not violate the dead body much more than the undertaker does. He extracts the last chance that the deceased has to physically aid his offspring. With their family's permission, several of my patients who died at home from potentially interesting diseases were personally autopsied by me in the undertaker's morgue.

The most horrible deaths were caused by fire. I stood by at a house fire while firemen extricated two charred children's' bodies. All I could do was pronounce them dead and soothe the family. Later, a woman with spastic cerebral palsy, whom I had treated, was trapped by a fire in her room. The best I could do was send her to the hospital by ambulance, but she died on the way.

One of my infant patients was carried, already dead, into my office. There were several close calls in the office, most of whom survived by immediate resuscitative measures or by subsequent hospital care. One very prominent citizen lay on my examining table in an extreme state. After admission to the hospital, he died from a massive coronary attack. During the later years of my general practice the hospitals became more medically oriented.

I was called to the scene of a few suicides. These were not as clean as they are today. Despondent people resorted to throat and wrist slashings, hanging, or both. The worst case was a regular patient, an elderly asthmatic, who took his life in a stable by combined hanging and wrist slashing. His family was well-known and faithful to me. His niece was my high school English teacher. From my experience, one who threatens suicide is apt to succeed, sooner or later.

One evening, at dusk, a couple called me and said they wanted to visit a friend, but could not get into the house. They could see the man sitting in a chair, but could not get his attention. I picked up the town constable. Upon arrival, I suspected that the man was dead. His neighbors did not know where the rest of the family were, so the policeman broke into the house. My patient was unequivocally dead.

On another occasion, I was requested to make a house call in the next township. There I found the largest human body I had ever seen. She had anasarca, which is a generalized edema, or swelling, of the entire body to an extreme degree. Her body was hard, and the skin was stretched so much that the pores were as large as nail holes and spaced an inch apart. A six-foot tape measure would not go all the way around her middle. She was barely alive. The hospital could not accommodate her because she would take two beds, side by side, and nobody could handle her. She was too large for an ambulance and we would need a flat-bed truck. Mercifully, she died at home in a few hours.

*Automobile insurance companies made bumper plates available
to identify the car of a physician.*

Several times I "heroically" resuscitated moribund and shocky patients in their home. The best agent in my black bag for such cases was adrenaline. For cardiac arrest, a long needle was quickly and unceremoniously plunged into the heart muscle and a good shot was administered. Sometimes it worked. One elderly lady, whom I had been treating in the office for a bad heart, was in just such a state when I screeched to a halt in her yard. The "stab in the heart" miraculously brought her around! Her family thought I was the brother of Jesus until she died in her sleep two days later.

In those days, highway accidents required a physician's services on the spot. One of the reasons for identifying a doctor's car was to allow him to be commandeered on the road when assistance was needed. We carried enough supplies to give first aid. By the early '50s the emergency squads were functioning better. Then it seemed that each time I received a frantic call from the State Police, especially along the New Jersey Turnpike, and risked my neck and arrest at breakneck speed, the patient had already been moved by an ambulance just before I arrived.

One reason the police called me so often was that the local barracks was on the same block as my office. Since I was handy, they often brought suspected drunken drivers to me for examination. I hated this chore, since I did not like drunks or the legalities involved. Occasionally, the subject would stop in later and want to know what I wrote on my report. Many times, I faced the possibility of revengeful physical harm, but it never happened.

Intoxication is an extremely prevalent condition and every doctor meets it face-to-face. Drunks can be funny or, sometimes, exasperating. Columbus had a weekender who would leave the local tavern, next to the police station, at closing time. He lived a mile from my office, which he passed while staggering home. He constantly muttered about beavers when he was "tanked." Often, in this state, he dropped in and demanded that I wash the wax out of his ears. I usually obliged to get rid of him. One late evening during Christmas season he came "beavering" along and banged on my front door. I knew who it was, but had to open the door to keep him from breaking the glass. As I did, he fell through the doorway and sprawled flat on his face. I hauled him up and steered him through the door to the waiting room. He fell again and wedged himself between the wall and the Christmas tree. The constable would not respond this time. I finally sobered him up a bit and sent him on his way.

The drunks were incurable, but there were other chronic problems with acute crises—-hernias were a prime example—-that could be cured by surgery if the patients would submit to it. People still thought hospitals were where you went to die. I became expert at manipulating all degrees of herniation back into place to prevent gangrene of the intestines. Most of these patients were repeaters. They depended upon trusses, which often were inadequate. My outstanding hernia patient was a carpenter whose hernia usually misbehaved in the middle of the night. It seemed as if one-third of his intestines slid through the inguinal canal, stretching the skin half way down his thigh! It might take an hour or two, but I always enticed the monster back here it belonged. He would not let me send him to a surgeon. His worst episode occurred when he fell all the way down the stair steps. This time I almost failed him.

Severe abdominal pain broke down resistance to hospitalization. When I diagnosed appendicitis there was no hesitation. One afternoon my father brought his next-door neighbor to me. He was a lifelong friend who was considered indestructible. I knew there was an abdominal catastrophe, which I suspected to be a ruptured organ. We admitted him to the chief general surgeon. His complaint was that he was having "false burps." He made belching noises and got relief, but the gas never came up. I saw this man daily in the hospital when I made rounds. He was not operated on for some medical reason. He died, much to my dismay. An autopsy revealed a ruptured peptic ulcer. This is my only experience with the aptly described false burp.

Less endangered, but more exasperating, were the hypochondriacs and psychosomatics. I could never understand why so many apparently healthy, hard working young people suffered so much from nervousness, indigestion, dizziness and palpitations. As I review my old office records,

I get the impression that at least twenty-five per cent of my patients were thus afflicted. Most of these people did not call me often. On the other hand, a few mature ladies hounded me constantly. Some called me every week, always for house calls. One had repeated spells of double heart rate, which I could control. The others were mostly imagination. I cannot count the times I was called back from some distant case for these ladies. Whenever I announced I would be away for a few days, the palpitater panicked. I would always have to see her just before I went and as soon as I got back. In my present orthopedic practice, most of the fakers are seeking compensation. My former patients wanted sympathy and attention. [24]

> *I have never forgotten a time when I was about ten years old, Uncle Morris bringing me into his office and allowing me to "assist" with a patient. The man had a foreign object in the bottom of his foot. Uncle Morris sat me on a foot stool, placed the man's heel on my shoulder and proceeded to remove the object with the big foot staring me right in the face. I'm not sure how the patient felt, but it certainly made me feel important. They just don't make doctors the way that they used to! (Letter written by Lorraine Woods for retirement party of Morris A. Robbins, M.D., January 22, 1995. Lorraine went on to become a Registered Nurse.)*

Pre-School Checkup Is Set at Columbus

Columbus, May 2—The summer roundup of pre-school children of Mansfield township for their physical checkup before entering Columbus school in the fall will be held tomorrow at 1.30 p. m. at the school.

Dr. Morris Robbins will be on hand to examine the children, assisted by Mrs. Lillian Brumfield, school nurse. The names of 36 children have been registered for the survey. Any others who will be five years old by October 15 are invited to attend.

Allentown Messenger

---

24   One female patient repeatedly showed up in the office with "prostate" problems. Despite careful explanations, she could not grasp that she had no prostate, and that her discomfort had a different cause.

I enjoyed being school physician for two townships. Mass sessions were held several times a year. A bonus was exposure to families, through the children, which kept me supplied with patients. Being an orthopedist at heart, I always looked for postural problems such as scoliosis (curvature of the spine). At present, the states mandate school screening for this condition.

The local P.T.A. engaged me as speaker one evening. I needed the blackboard, so the janitor helped me move it across the stage. He had only a left arm, and I a right. The audience began to laugh, especially when reminded that it took two of us to make one man!

The Robbins family, 1950

Betty and I were blessed with two children. With the first-born, Dorothy, we had to leave the Easter service for the hospital. Betty's obstetrician died a couple of weeks before, so we had to take pot luck. One of my respected general practice colleagues officiated at the last minute, and there were no problems. Bill came along according to protocol, with the new O.B. man in complete charge. There were other small children in the area, so there was no lack of playmates. In fact, things got pretty thick at times.

One afternoon Bill and I were home alone when he fell off the swing. He whimpered and held his arm. It looked all right, but he acted as if he were going to faint. All I could think of was head injury. When his mother returned, I X-rayed his arm, which was intact. Doctors have difficulty caring for close relatives, for emotional reasons. Nature, rather than legislation, causes us to seek help from our colleagues. Many years later I was forced to set Bill's arm from another accident, when no one else was available.

The irony of general practice in those days was that the worse the weather the more house calls we had to make. When it was not fit for man nor beast the doctor had to go out! Blizzards and fog were the worst. If I had not been so well acquainted with the territory, I could not have found my way in some of the dense night fogs. I used a spotlight on my car. One foggy night I had to visit a man who lived along the highway. I left the spotlight on when I went into the house, hoping the shaft of light would prevent someone from slamming into my car.

Blizzards were dangerous because of freezing cold and whiteouts. Landmarks disappeared. I have slid into ditches where it required a tractor to extricate my vehicle. Once, on my way to a call, I had to follow the telephone wires rather than the road. The drifts were so large that. in one place. the plows had deviated a bit but I could not detect that. The front half of the Ford buried itself in the drift and stuck fast. My only recourse was to set out on foot with my black bag. It was so windy and slippery that I fell down several times. but I completed the call. Another snowstorm caused me to get lost two miles from home! Even the hills seemed to change shape. and I got home by divine guidance.

The Jeep

Eventually. I bought a surplus military Jeep. It was repainted. but the Air Force star was still outlined on the hood. beneath the paint. I made a sedan body for it to give me some protection in bad weather. In a snowstorm it was wonderful under foot, but when things got bad, I was unable to see through the windshield or the side windows. On many a sloppy day I used it for house calls. I would drive right to the edge of the house steps, so my feet would not touch the ground.

I often towed a disabled vehicle or helped a farmer carry heavy objects across the field. In addition to its utility, the Jeep was fun to drive. Sometimes I did crazy things with it. One veteran showed me how to slide it along sidewise through a mud hole, but I could never muster enough courage to try it. Only twice did I get stuck in it. by stalling the engine and hanging up both axles at once.

One stormy summer day I had just driven my daughter home from her grandmother's. An urgent house call was waiting for me. A half mile from my house, as I crossed the railroad tracks, everything suddenly turned black and the Jeep windows popped out with a mighty roar and shudder. I thought a train had struck me. Later. the neighbors told me they saw a small twister down by the tracks at the instant I was there.

Joe Schultze was a former Prussian army officer who later served in the American forces during World War II. He had a service station in town where he used to help me make parts for experimental arms. Being an excellent cook. he often fed me when Betty was away. Joe also had a Jeep onto which German war prisoners had built a sedan body for the personal use of General Mark Clark. One icy morning my Jeep would not start. It was parked down a grade behind my house. I called Joe. who brought his beloved rig to give me a tow-start.

On the way up the hill mine started but his stalled. We exchanged towing positions, and I proceeded to pull the "General" out to the street. Again. visibility was practically nonexistent through my rear window. Over the engine noise I thought I heard Joe shout, "Give her hell, Doc!" I did just that. and took off down the slippery street to get him started. His Jeep started to fishtail at the end of the tow rope. and I feared Joe had fainted. When I stopped, he was running toward me, jumping up and down, shouting. "Mein cheep. mein cheep!" He had not gotten into his vehicle when I started pulling. Thankfully, our friendship survived.

The Jeep played another spectacular role in my practice. A farmer's cows were getting sick. His son came to my office with skin lesions which I correctly diagnosed as human anthrax. The State went into immediate action and found an epidemic of anthrax in the farm animals. The family was furious, but also scared enough to allow me to treat their son. I had orders to use strict quarantine technique and the family was forbidden to leave their property. I went to the farm every day for a week, in the open vehicle, and gave the boy penicillin shots. He stood by the Jeep while I injected him, without my setting foot on the ground.

Two doors from my house lived Dr. Ryland Croshaw, the local veterinarian. We were about the same age, and both natives of the area. He specialized in cows, of which there were multitudes on the surrounding farms. Of course, we compared notes concerning our respective professions. At times, I would ride with him. More than once we went in his car to answer calls where we were both needed. He would head for the barn and I for the house.

One day we should have done this, but the barn and house call did not synchronize. When I arrived to attend to the children the mother informed me that she had a sick puppy and that "Doc" Croshaw had just left. I gave the puppy a baby aspirin and he recovered. On another occasion I did a sperm count on my cousin's standardbred stud, which was not siring properly. I found it low and told Jack[25] what I would do for a man. He followed my advice, with a fruitful outcome. I have no idea how many times Ryland turned the tables on me because he never confessed.

Hospital life was more than patients. We were kept on our toes by clinico-pathological conferences and Staff meetings. Most Staff business was handled by the Executive Committee. In the general meeting we always discussed deaths, exchanged ideas and criticized diagnoses and treatments. Following the war, we acquired a professional pathologist from Philadelphia, Dr. John Bauer, an erudite and thorough scholar. His discussions of autopsy findings were so complete and complicated, and he was so intellectually honest, that we often did not understand the exact cause of death. He stayed with Burlington County until he retired.

The hospital dining room was delightful. Any doctor on duty at meal time was entitled to a sit-down meal served by a waiter. The head table was occupied by the Medical Superintendent (Dr. Summey), Dr. Bauer and Dr. Luis Viteri (the Chief of Medicine). Occasionally one of us would be invited and honored to eat at the captain's table. When the hospital began to modernize, the first change was the dining room. It was replaced by a cafeteria, and the charm disappeared.

Although patients were generally appreciative and loyal, there were instances where they turned on me. I seldom missed office hours or house

---

25   Jack Smith, Jr. (1922-1988) well-known harness racer and trainer; recognized as one of the nation's top conditioners of young horses.

calls because of personal illness. Community doctors were so constantly exposed to a variety of infectious diseases that we would suffer some of the symptoms, but rarely be put out of commission. There were times when we could hardly drag along, but we were supposed to be heroes. Occasionally the flu bug would get to me enough to make me refuse a night call. This never sat well with the patients or their families. There were other doctors available, but I was not supposed to get sick! People would forgive poor results, but not refusal to respond.

Medical life was not all work, although it often seemed that way. We rented a place at the shore for a week each summer. If necessary, I would commute to the office. We took the Jeep to use on the beach for fishing and exploring. It could creep along the sand, in four-wheel drive, at a walking pace. We could beachcomb and transport tiring children while the driver walked alongside. I believe the old-style military Jeep was the ultimate American sports car, except for high speed racing. We even picked blueberries from it, with the windshield down, without setting foot on the ground.

Dr. Robbins and nurse Olive Mattola

My wonderful office nurse, Olive Mottola, had a machinist husband, Harry, who did a lot of work on my prosthetic research projects. He was a Hudson automobile buff, and had been a pit mechanic at the Indianapolis Speedway. He tried his best to sell me a Hudson Hornet, one of the top "muscle cars." It was too rich for my blood and a little too large for my needs. Harry tricked me into opening one up on the highway. When the telephone poles became blurry, I backed off at 108 miles-per-hour!

Goldy Bryan, whose mother died that first winter, and I became bosom pals. In warm weather we tried to take a trip to the shore every Wednesday afternoon. He owned a seaside cottage and a boat. Before returning we ate a dozen or two raw clams apiece. This was welcome relaxation from practice.

One night, after a house call, two fat raccoons waddled in front of me, one in each rut of the sandy road. They claimed right-of-way and I followed them for a while, lighting their way with my headlights. Foxes, skunks, snakes and other creatures crossed paths with me at night.

Dogs often challenged me when I entered their territory. With my heavy black bag and prosthesis, I managed to ward them off. The little dogs could be diverted with the bag. The bigger ones were offered my fiberglass arm and they clamped down on it, at which instant I would punch their underbellies and cool them off.

The fiberglass interchangeable hand of one prosthesis

I continued to experiment with mechanical arms. Fiberglass was coming onto the scene, and I quickly took advantage of it. My latest limbs are still part fiberglass, especially in the sockets. I made some 'glass braces for patients. From Seattle, Washington, a company marketed rolls of cloth containing twenty percent fiberglass and eighty percent polyester. By soaking this material in a secret formula containing ether and acetone, a variety of braces and casts were fabricated right in the office. These were more durable and water resistant than plaster-of-Paris. The initial odor was awesome and the danger of explosion was present, but adequate forced ventilation prevented trouble. Patients accepted some of the devices I made for them, then. This material became the basis for my own prostheses.[26]

Dr. Croshaw was an amateur carpenter and stone mason. He built roads, dams, spillways, buildings and farm machinery. One of his projects

---

26   Eventually, he molded a plaster model of Betty's left hand, and attached it to his device. That was the hand he used for surgery, because it fit in a surgical glove. Both literally and figuratively, Betty was Morris' other hand.

was a lake which he made on property he bought in the pine forest. I was with him one night after he had closed the dam and was waiting for the water to begin trickling over the spillway. As exciting as this was, the heavens were exceeding it. The northern lights were playing a spectacular show across ninety degrees of the sky, stopping directly overhead. Neither of us had witnessed anything like this. His project is now the borough of Hampton Lakes.

> Sunday morning, and also installed Dr. Morris Robbins as an elder of the church and member of the session. Mrs Harry W George of 51 West

Allentown Messenger, Feb. 10, 1949

> a motion picture on the heart at the meeting of the Columbus Grange held last Friday evening. Dr. Morris Robbins, township physician, also spoke on diseases of the heart. The following members of the Man f

Allentown Messenger, Mar. 18, 1948

> College, Trenton. Dr. and Mrs. Morris Robbins and children Dorothy Ann and William are spending a two-week vacation at the Lippincott cottage in Surf City. Mr and Mrs Frank D

Allentown Messenger, Sept. 24, 1953

Editor's note: Doc fails to mention that, in addition to a busy practice, he was much in demand for local committees, was serving as an Elder in his church, and was a frequent speaker at community functions. The local papers reported his every move, including vacations and dinner invitations.

Chapter 11
ORTHOPEDIC TRAINING

During my general practice I attended clinics and seminars at the world-renowned Kessler Institute for Rehabilitation in West Orange, New Jersey. Dr. Henry Kessler, who was head of the organization, traveled extensively for the government during the war. Second in command was another orthopedic surgeon, Dr, Carl Arthur Maxwell, with whom I became friendly because some of his relatives lived in my practice area and had been my patients. In 1954, nine years after I started in Columbus, Arthur telephoned me. He was leaving the Institute, and invited me to apply for his position. I was sorely tempted because of my interest in the place and its world-wide reputation. The disturbing aspect was the necessity of moving to northern New Jersey. Apparently, the job was not full-time, and I was still a general practitioner. An interview was arranged, and Dr. Kessler asked me what I wanted to do. I told him I really wanted an orthopedic residency, so I could become an orthopedic specialist. He gave me a residency in The Hospital for Crippled Children, where he worked, in Newark.

Dr. John B. Gearren, of Bordentown, has been appointed school physician, to fill the vacancy created when Dr. Morris Robbins resigned to take a post-graduate course in orthopedic surgery at the Hospital of Crippled Children, Newark. Mrs. Isabel Scott, of Vincentown, will continue as school nurse.

Allentown Messenger, Aug. 26, 1954

My new position called for drastic changes, both for my patients and family. There was no doctor available to take over my practice, so two evenings a week I would see a few office patients when I came home. House and emergency calls were no longer possible. Furthermore, my wife found it

81

necessary to go back to teaching home economics. The grandparents took care of our children during the day. I had to get up at five-thirty to be at the hospital by eight. Many times, I left the hospital late because of unfinished chores. The on-call schedule was the same as internship.

COLUMBUS

Mrs. Morris Robbins will teach home economics in the Florence Township High School when classes start in September.

Allentown Messenger

Before my reversion to student status, I was elected President of The Burlington County Medical Society. Medical affairs were going along rather smoothly at the time, so I kept the position. As a result, I was not much more than a presiding officer. The only distinction I can remember was my new nickname, "The Resident President." The biggest problem during my term was the introduction of Salk vaccine to the public. It was supported by The March of Dimes, and people demanded it before it was completely ready for general use. Fortunately, it worked. with its use poliomyelitis became almost extinct, and a large and important part of orthopedic practice disappeared.

In medical school I learned the theory of medicine. General practice taught human nature, especially during illness. In Newark, along with technical training, I became "street-wise" about competition and medical politics. In the country our policy was to "live and let live," since we were scarce and dependent upon each other. In the city I was confronted with the specter of professional jealousy.

The greatest personal discomfort was my relationship with the other residents. They were young, inexperienced and ambitious. Because of my age and handicap, I had difficulty getting my share of operative work. They were glad to let me do the floor work, but resented my competition in the operating room. A few of the attending surgeons treated me the same way. Younger staff members were more friendly and eager to share my experience. I was relegated to the "lesser" surgeons who also felt repressed by the overbearing top brass. The plastic surgeon favored me and I learned a lot of reconstructive technique from him. There was little didactic teaching in this residency, but plenty of labor.

There were still alternate routes to acceptable orthopedic training leading to certification. The hospital where I worked was considered a children's' orthopedic center, but the staff found it a convenient place to take their adult cases as well. An offshoot of this tendency was a comprehensive study of paralyzed people, especially paraplegics. Dr. Kessler had a contract with the United Mine Workers, and many West Virginia coal miners received spinal cord injuries. They came to us in large enough numbers to make this an outstanding part of the program for me. After a year I had a choice of transferring to the Veterans' Hospital in Brooklyn or Metropolitan on Welfare Island. Instead, I enrolled in the Graduate School of Medicine of the University of Pennsylvania. This institution and the Hospital for Crippled Children no longer exist.

A full academic year at Penn, where I was previously rejected for regular medical school, fulfilled my academic needs. Dissection was emphasized, and we operated on cadavers. Affiliation with most of the outstanding facilities in Philadelphia and Wilmington made the year worthwhile. The DuPont Institute in Wilmington and Shriner's Hospital in Philadelphia continued to be utilized after I returned to private practice.

When I started graduate school, I transferred my general practice and office to Dr. Lawrence McCay. This relieved me of further obligations to my old patients and gave me time to study.

Preceptorship had been an acceptable method of training for a specialty from the beginning. It took twice as long as the residency route but it was more practical and patient-orientated. One man was the boss, but colleagues were encountered in the hospitals, similar to a residency. A preceptee, or apprentice, could become a full partner later. Dr. E. Vernon Davis had just become certified by the American Board of Orthopedic Surgery, and I chose to be his apprentice. He had appointments in Burlington County, Cooper and others. Orthopedists were still riding the circuit because there were few of us in those days.

Once again, I was working in familiar clinics, assisting at operations, making rounds and caring for office patients. The only difference from before was that he was boss and I had to answer to him. Some of my old patients came because I was there and my future clientele increased. I worked for peanuts I " so my wife had to keep on teaching.

A few months after I went with Dr. Davis, Betty and I received the horrifying news that the State had condemned our house and office to make way for a new highway through town. We only had six-week's notice. That also meant that Dr. McCay would lose the office.

His father, Albert, was State Senator from our district, and an old family friend. He helped us find a new home in Delanco, along the Delaware River and next-door to his own. The new place cost more than we received for the old house, so we had to take a mortgage.

. *"...I was notified by the New Jersey State Highway Commission that my property in Columbus stands in the way of the proposed new Route 206[27], and that I must vacate by September 30, 1956. The right of way negotiator has set his offer for my property at $25,000.... Since this bombshell exploded after I had returned to practice only an only, following two years of study for the specialty which I am now practicing, I find it necessary to borrow every dollar that will be needed to buy another property pending settlement by the State."* (letter from Morris A. Robbins, M.D. to the Union National Bank and Trust Company, June 26, 1956)

COLUMBUS
Dr. and Mrs. Morris Robbins and family moved Friday to their new home in Delanco.

Allentown Messenger, Oct. 4, 1956

It was equivalently distant from Burlington County and Cooper hospitals. My apprenticeship continued for three years. I worked as hard as ever, but night and house calls were scarce, and the routine was healthier. The office was in Camden, near The Cooper Hospital. On our operating mornings I went directly to the respective hospitals. From there we both went to the office. Hospital rounds were part of the program. When Dr. Davis was away, I was in full charge. In order for this arrangement to work, my Cooper appointment was changed to Assistant Orthopedic Surgeon. I held this position until I resigned after opening an office in Burlington to practice on my own. Since my boss was Chief of Orthopedic Surgery at several hospitals, my training was satisfactory as far as I was concerned.

---

27   the house was moved to a lot on Route 206 behind its former site.

The Thunderbird; in this photo, the deformed right hand and prothesis are visible.

Financially, things were difficult for five years. In addition to the house mortgage and upkeep there were hospital dues, donations, hospital building programs, community requests for money and payments on my new car. Harry Mottola switched to Ford when Hudson went out of business. He placed a new 1956 Thunderbird in my yard and arranged for financing. He was an optimist and insisted that, although I was "broke" I had potential because of my profession. This was the best automotive investment I ever made. At this writing I am still driving that car. It is thirty-seven years old and has exceeded a quarter million miles.[28]

Dr. Davis was very active in the politics of organized medicine. He faithfully attended the annual conventions of The American Academy of Orthopedic Surgeons and usually took me with him. I met the "big wheels " and was exposed to the frontiers of the specialty.

We pioneered in the early hip replacement procedures which preceded the now popular total implants. We also did a lot of spinal surgery, especially fusions. In our day we tried to alter the original joint anatomy to encourage repair. Today, these operations are usually discarded in favor of total artificial replacements for bad joints and metal internal bracing for spines. These are quick fixes but they are running into trouble with breakdowns and delayed infection. We employed bone grafts and long-term plaster casts, and we seemed to have fewer complications than the present methods.

---

28   The 1956 Thunderbird is still in the Robbins family.

My apprenticeship was completed in 1959. It was the custom to sit for Part One of the certification examinations at the completion of the training period. I did this at Georgetown University. I passed the examination and was especially complimented by one of the examiners. Now I was a partially certified full-fledged orthopedic surgeon. The next requirement was two years of independent practice before taking the final Part Two.

Chapter 12
EARLY ORTHOPEDIC PRACTICE

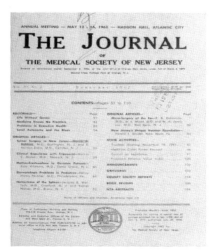

The article can be read in the Harvard Library collection
of State Medical Journals, https://guides.library.harvard.edu/

While training with Dr. Davis, I reviewed our spinal surgery and wrote a scientific article for publication. It was accepted by the Journal of the Medical Society of New Jersey and appeared in 1962, with Dr. Davis as co-author. I am sure his political prominence helped, because I have never been able to "crack" a medical journal since. Medical literature seems to be dominated by the faculty of teaching institutions. Full-time clinicians, who have the most practical experience, do not have time or facilities to investigate and write in a matter acceptable to the top-notch "refereed" professional journals. So much valuable information is lost when clinicians retire because it is only recorded in their patient records, which are not public. The speakers at conventions and seminars are the professors or their subordinates. The full-time healers only listen. Often what they hear is useless as far as improving medical practice is concerned. Academe seems to rule the profession.

During World War II, Dr. Davis and some practitioners from Cape May were stationed in San Francisco. While there, they organized a new hospital to be built in Cape May Court House, New Jersey. It was completed after the war, and Dr. Davis was the Chief of the Department of Orthopedic Surgery. Dr. Winfield Betts, of Medford, assisted him for years. Eventually, I was allowed to participate. Just before I left the Camden office, Dr. Davis resigned from the new Burdette Tomlin Memorial Hospital and I was appointed in his place. Thus, my initial full-privilege orthopedic surgery assignment was in a hospital ninety miles from home!

has an appointment with

Morris A. Robbins, M.D.
313 W. Broad Street
Burlington, N.J. 08016
Phone: (609) 386-0313

Date _____ Time _____

In fairness to others please call *(24 hours in advance)* if you must change
or cancel your appointment.

Another part time orthopedist friend offered me space in his office in Beverly. I stayed with Dr. William P. Mulford for fifteen months. In that period, I joined some doctors and lawyers from Burlington in the construction of a professional complex named the Bridge Plaza Professional Center. We occupied it in the spring of 1960. I am the only member of the original group still there.[29]

Under construction: Bridge Plaza Professional Center, Burlington, New Jersey

There was no difficulty acquiring patients. While I was in Camden a few of my professional and business friends urged me to return to the Burlington

---

29   He retired and sold the office in 1994.

County riverfront area to practice. I knew they were sincere, and they proved it by referring patients regularly.

Doc in his Burlington office, with his ever-present pipe

The new Burlington office was reminiscent of my Columbus one. My next-door neighbor in the complex was a good radiologist. We had an inner door between us, so I could handle fracture follow-up in the office. We were never able to recapture the golden hour of fracture management, but our follow-up facilities were excellent. Although I designed the office to handle minor surgery, it was seldom used for this. The original fiberglass cast people went out of business, so the elaborate ventilation system to remove ether and acetone fumes was superfluous. The basement was designed for use by a physical therapist and a brace maker, but was not so utilized until twenty-three years later. The extra-wide doors, ramp and friction-free traffic for stretchers are utilized fully. Emergency squads bring patients right to the office when necessary.

Doc's appointment as Special Deputy Sheriff

The hospital clinics were still at their peak. In return for our charity work the administration let us use the facilities for private patients outside of clinic hours. Many patients were examined and treated by me in the outpatient section when I was already at the hospital or not having office hours. Although handy, this became a nuisance by interfering with scheduled inpatient activities. People took advantage of the constant availability and facilities thus afforded. Lately, since the advent of third- party medical benefits and elimination of the clinics, the hospitals charge for this service. The role of the hospital has gradually changed from an easily available, cheap place to see one's doctor to a business-like, cost conscious, highly regulated system of red tape, computerized records and rather cold, scientific but effective diagnosis and therapy. One advantage of this change has been the rebirth of importance and utilization of the doctor's private office.

When hospitals were smaller and more independent, they were the domain of a few strong men, or czars. The chiefs ran their departments with an iron hand. Competition was discouraged. Newcomers were considered assistants, whose role was to help fill beds and do the menial work, but not to interfere with the chief. He had "his" mornings reserved for his operations, and his anticipated or actual schedule was not to be violated. For example, all except emergency orthopedic operations had to be scheduled for the allotted time on the proper days of the week. Elective cases were admitted with this in mind. The worst part was that an assistant's operations only could be scheduled the day before, after the chief knew what he was going to do and had finished his cases. Several times I was unable to operate and had to send my patients home, to return the next week. Under the new utilization regulations, such a thing is unheard of today.

During the first two years of my independent practice I studied constantly to prepare for the second part of the examination. I had to maintain my work to make ends meet, and study at night, as in medical school. At the designated time I flew to Chicago where I lived in the Palmer House for a week. The written part of the examination was multiple choice, a system I never liked. The questions always had two possibly correct answers, one being "always" or "never" and the other "usually" or "sometimes." After eighteen years' experience in clinical medicine, I picked the "usually" answer, because nothing is black vs. white in medicine—-only shades of gray. They probably wanted the answer that reflected the teacher-to-student approach, to give it back as the book says. At any rate, I received a grade of sixty-five when seventy was passing. The five or six oral examinations were given in different subjects, each by a senior academician and a junior, jointly.

There was no stage fright and I answered in the language of a consultant, according to my convictions. When I returned home and the results carne, I had flunked the very subjects in which I was most interested and experienced, namely biomechanics, braces and limbs, and children's' orthopedics! I received a grade of sixty-five on this section, too. They invited me to try again the following year.

After another year of intensive study, I flew to Miami Beach to repeat the procedure. Before the sessions started, I met one of my professors, who expressed great surprise that they let me appear for the examinations! The procedure was the same as in Chicago. When I entered a booth for an oral the younger man whispered to the older one, "There he is!" These two episodes made me apprehensive. When the grades came, I had another sixty-five on the written and flunked two orals. The failed subjects were different this time. I passed the ones I flunked previously and flunked the ones I passed before!

By this time, I was fed up, and resolved to forget about certification and go about my business. I was too old and poor to stop my practice again and seek another residency, as I was advised to do to maintain my eligibility. I wanted to remain loyal to my patients. Some of my specialist friends had trained and never taken the examinations. Dr. Charles Schwartz, who cared for me back in the '30s, never passed his boards because the examiners hated his father and told Charlie he would never make it! I knew I was not slated for certification, in spite of my good showing in Part I. Why had they let me proceed to Part II?

Without board certification one can never become a Diplomate of the American Academy of Orthopedic Surgeons, the hub of organized orthopedic surgery. but can attend their meetings as a paying guest and receive their literature. I sought a haven in the American College of Surgeons, but their response was that I did not go through the student candidate ranks with them and take a residency approved by them. They stopped me in my tracks! To add insult to injury, the local orthopedic clubs would not consider me for membership because I did not pass my boards. As a result, I have never belonged to any specialty organization.

One possible reason for these disappointments is that, while I was serving my preceptorship, the program was dismantled. Authorities claimed it was not effective training. I disagree. In my forced opinion, certification has been used by the politically powerful specialists to maintain control over their closed shops and personal interests. Without official blessing, I have remained a loner and have done my best to care for my patients and keep on top of the important developments in my specialty.

Dictating Equipment Donated By Auxiliary 7/9/62

New dictating equipment for physicians' use at Zur-
brugg Memorial Hospital, Riverside, is put to use.
The equipment, including typewriter, was donated
by the Riverton Junior Auxiliary to the hospital.
Utilizing the donated items are (from left, seated)
Mrs. Alfred Johnson, medical secretary, and Dr.

Hammell Shipps, chief attending gynecologist and
obstetrician. Also (from left, standing) Mrs. Emma
Bower of Riverton, Mrs. Floyd Schulz, auxiliary
president, and Dr. Morris Rabbins, assistant orthe-
pedist. (Times Staff Photo by Brown)

Following these set-backs, Dr. Oswald Carlander became Chief-of-Staff at Zurbrugg Memorial Hospital in Riverside, close to my office and home. He was also Chief of Orthopedic Surgery. He deliberately withheld my appointment there until he acquired his new position. His personality was similar to mine, and he had no grandiose ideas of political power. I was appointed and subsequently built up a local clientele through Zurbrugg. He let me do anything I wanted, "just so you don't get into trouble in the operating room." Zurbrugg[30] quickly became my main hospital, although I continued to work in the others.

Insurance companies and lawyers began to use me for consultations, treatment and expert testimony in court. I gradually began to doubt the practical value of certification in community medicine and the fairness of the orthopedic brass. Years later, the professor who wondered why they let me take the second part of the Boards admitted that they were unfair!

I was spreading myself rather thin, so I resigned from Cooper, since it was too far away for my patients. For seventeen years following my internship I worked there for nothing, paid my yearly dues and assessments, and attended numerous meetings because they were mandatory. Now I was my own man again and, being in my middle 40s, it was about time!

---

30   Zurbrugg Memorial Hospital closed in the 1990s, and has since been torn down.

Occasionally, someone will confidentially ask me whether I did the operating myself or guided an assistant to do it for me. This is a natural uncertainty and I am not insulted by it. By using ingenuity and concentration, I always was the operating surgeon. My assistants fulfilled their standardized role but they did not do the operating - I let them sew up and apply dressings, as they were supposed to, but I did the definitive surgery myself. As far as I know, no one has ever taken a picture of me operating. There are many first hand witnesses, however. I also do my mechanical and craftsman work myself, with only occasional assistance. The prosthesis is the physical reason for my success. '

Chapter 13

CHIEF ORTHOPEDIC SURGEON

At Burdette Tomlin my patients were admitted in my name, but the referring doctor, usually a general surgeon, cooperated in daily care. I operated before the clinic session. Post-operatively I would make the two-hundred-mile round trip every chance I got. A house physician always assisted me at operation, as part of his job. For over twenty years this routine continued, and it was the epitome of the circuit-riding surgical practice. The clinic was as large as the office sessions at home. Dr. Betts stayed with me until he switched from private practice to emergency medicine in Mount Holly. I also attended Medical Staff meetings once a month, which meant that I did not arrive home until after midnight. To ease the burden, I changed the clinic to Friday afternoon and stayed overnight at the shore. This allowed me to make rounds the day after surgery and eliminated the pressure of operating at Zurbrugg the next morning. My wife could then go with me to enjoy the outing and share in the driving.

At Burlington County Memorial Hospital things did not go so well for me; I was undoubtedly obligated to the chief and was in no position to openly compete with him. It was a naturally ideal place for me to practice since my patients were accustomed to going there for their needs. My patient load there was minor compared to his and he continued to dominate the scene. I believe he made a mistake in failing to groom me as an equal coworker and possible successor to his position. (He was eleven years older than I.) After I left his office, he took in two new partners who were added to the staff. Certified orthopedic surgeons began to appear out of the woodwork, with no previous connections to the hospital or the chief. They were too aggressive and active for me to compete against. I realized I was licked when a new operating suite was opened and the lockers in the dressing room were assigned to everyone but me! My last operation at that hospital was on a Saturday afternoon as I assisted the surgical resident with a hip pinning. In its drive to become a fancy medical center the hospital outgrew me and I became a stranger there. I like smaller and more personal institutions, and prefer cooperation to direct competition.

See complete presentation in the Appendix

When things started going sour for me at Burlington County I was approached by a part-time radiologist at the hospital, Dr. Amerigo George'. He was a founder of a proposed hospital in Hammonton, and he recognized my predicament. He is a good man who is genuinely interested in other doctors and wants them to succeed. He invited me to join the founders' group and to help get the Kessler Memorial Hospital going. A second boost came from a young assistant administrator at Zurbrugg, Richard Sherman. He was leaving to become the administrator at Kessler, and he also wanted me to go with him. At this time the so-called hospital was merely an office, and the building was not yet started. I took both of these men at their word.

By the time the new hospital opened, other orthopedic surgeons suddenly appeared. By virtue of their connections with the local doctors and board members, they tried to take over the Department of Orthopedic Surgery. But I dug in and built up a practice in the area, even though it meant constant hundred-mile round trips, day and night. These fellows appointed themselves Chief, in turn, but none of them stayed very long.

The majority of the staff were young immigrants. Only one or two surgeons wanted to do fractures, so I had no real competition. We started out with a house staff of foreign graduates who were willing to work like interns to get started. For a few years these men made good assistants. They gradually established local practices and drifted away from student status. After their departure, some continued to assist at surgery for a fee. The problem, at that time, was to convince patients and third parties to pay for surgical assistance. It was not ethical for the surgeon to pay an assistant out of his own fee. It was none of my business what they charged except when an insurance company complained that the assistant charged more than the surgeon!

Eventually my immediate successor in partnership with Dr. Davis came on the staff. Dr. Hassan Kekavat is an American trained Iranian, and his kinship with the local doctors grew. Thus, he began to share the work in Hammonton. He did not leave, so we formed a department. Because of my seniority, I was appointed Chief of Orthopedic Surgery.

My functions as Chief were low-key, similar to Dr. Carlander's. I acted only when necessary. My services were occasionally required in disputes between the volatile staff members and in requests to carry out new procedures.

The new hospital functioned as Burlington County did before it began to modernize. Our relationship with the doctors and nurses was easy and informal. We saw people in the outpatient section as a courtesy of the administration. There was no need for either of us to maintain a branch office in Hammonton. Frequent social events contributed to goodwill in the hospital family. We orthopedists covered for each other when necessary, but did not otherwise share patients.

In the late '60s Dr. Davis began to relinquish his heavy involvement in Zurbrugg and I was appointed Chief of Orthopedic Surgery. By this time Dr. Carlander had retired. This was my home territory which I could cover without the hassle of traveling. The department contained more members than at Kessler. For the others, Zurbrugg was secondary, but for me it was primary. Zurbrugg grew, but did not become impersonal or unwieldy. All departments were improved, so more difficult procedures became practical. In addition to my orthopedic duties at Zurbrugg, I took my turn as

Chief-of-Staff and on various committees. The Executive Committee, on which I served several years, influences medical affairs.

An entirely new city of Willingboro, the largest in the county, developed close to Riverside, where Zurbrugg is located. As our plant expanded it was utilized heavily by new doctors from there and elsewhere. Medical politics became more democratic and controversial. Competition for beds became more acute, and tempers often reached the boiling point. In an effort to control this situation, a new Division of Surgery was created to unify the various surgical specialties for political reasons. I was elected Chairman of the Surgical Division for an indefinite term. I was the "peacemaker" again.

"Dear Morris: You gave me the thrill of my life when I received your letter. God knows I am happy to hear that you and yours are healthy and well. I won't ever forget you...." (Letter from E. Vernon Davis, M.D., Feb. 27, 1979)

Doc had a reputation for being able to explain complex medical issues in terms that could be understood easily by a non-medical listener or patient. Just as he had done in Columbus, he gave talks in a variety of local venues. The Camden Courier-Post newspaper made good use of that talent by including him in a series of columns published under the title "Ask the Experts", several of which appear here.

Boning up on medicine

Growing pains

Q. I have a 13-year-old son who is very active. He has pain in his right leg usually in the calf. As a rule the pain is worse at night. I give him aspirin and I rub his calf muscle and he gets better. He also has unexplained fever for short periods of time. But he's not ill. He's been in the hospital a few times and has had tests but these were all negative. This has been going on since he was two. What do you think? The tests included tests for rheumatic fever.

A. In light of the fact that he's apparently been well checked over and nothing was found to be wrong, there might be no problem other than overuse of the muscle in the leg.

You've heard of the old idea of growing pains. That idea became unpopular. People thought there wasn't any such thing. But lately physicians are beginning to talk about it again.

If things get worse you should continue having your son checked by a physician.

— DR. ROBBINS

COURIER-POST, Wednesday, March 12, 1980

Dr. Henry K. Sherk
Head
Division of Orthopedic Surgery
Cooper Medical Center

Dr. Morris A. Robbins
Chief
Department of Orthopedic Surgery
Zurbrugg Memorial Hospital

Hurt shoulder muscle

Q. In December I was painting the house and was moving a ladder. I hurt the shoulder muscle on the right side of my chest. I've had a lot of pain. The small veins stand out visibly in the area and there is some swelling. I don't have sharp pain but I do ache, especially at night. My family doctor is giving me medication and electric shock treatment to the muscle. I don't seem to be getting any better. What should I do? Is my condition dangerous?

A. I advise light exercise to the point of pain. But stop before the muscle starts to bind up on you. Light exercise would include doing your normal household tasks. When you do something that brings that pain on, stop there. Also, don't lift the ladder any more.

I think you should also have more intensive physiotherapy than you are getting. You should be having massage. Your condition is probably not dangerous — just annoying at this stage. It won't cause any permanent damage, such as tearing, unless you did it in the first place. You probably did not do this.

— DR. ROBBINS

Pain in leg

Q. My 60-year-old husband has been complaining of pain in his right leg. The pain goes from his buttock down to his right groin then down his leg to the ankle muscle. It began in May of 1979 when he lifted something heavy and felt something give in his back. He's been hospitalized. He's had multiple X-rays, a myelogram and a bone scan. The results of all of the studies have been normal. His doctor has prescribed treatments (including whirlpool treat-

TONIGHT AND TOMORROW

Tonight's Ask the Experts evening panel for Teens will answer questions about women's sports and physical fitness. If you have a question, call 590-0351 tonight between 6:30 p.m. and 8 p.m. and Ask The Experts.

98

Dr. Morris A. Robbins
Chief
Department of Orthopedic Surgery
Zurbrugg Memorial Hospital

the proper specialist, such as an oral surgeon or ear, nose and throat physician.
— DR. ZEIDMAN

Bunion

Q. I have a bunion on my left foot. I've had it for several years. It bothers me when I wear certain shoes. I'm a middle-aged woman of average build. I don't do any work other than housework. I'm going to the hospital to have the bunion operated on. Will the surgery be successful?

A. Usually yes. There are several ways to operate on a bunion and the aftercare and the amount of time you have to stay off your foot depends somewhat on the kind of operation. But since there will be surgery on only one foot you will be able to walk with crutches and on your good leg immediately. But it will take about three weeks before you should put weight on the foot that has been operated on.

In about six weeks you should be able to bear weight fairly well on the foot that surgery was performed on. Then the foot should gradually get better.

There will be some pain and your foot will swell. Certain operations shorten the toe but the motion should be restored. You'll have trouble for a while with pushing off at the end of a step.

Usually the patient finds the results of the operation rewarding.
— DR. ROBBINS

Doc was a regular contributor to the "Ask the Experts",
column in the Camden Courier-Post

An outstanding vacation activity for several years was voluntary service in the Merchant Marine. I started riding a coastal oil tanker where I learned some navigation and seamanship. Later I transferred to a river tug boat which I often had the pleasure of piloting. The oil transport company eventually was sold and my marine activities ceased.

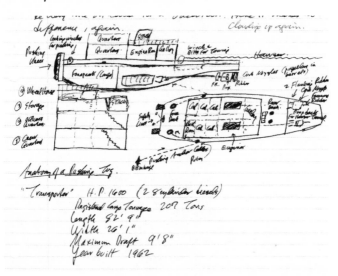

"4/6/79: Woke up at 5:30, sailing on the Chesapeake Bay. The wind was up, so we cut loose of the stern of the barge, allowed the already secured hawser to play out, and proceeded to tow the barge aft. Waves splashed against the barge's deck house and over the deck. The radio kept warning of gale force winds. Some of the tugs had anchored to ride it out. I had the privilege of seeing the first jewel-like point of the rising sun across the water, while waiting for the barge to behave at the end of the tightening tow line. As we progressed, the wind and waves worsened. Chris[31] reduced speed and we did not do badly. It was difficult to walk in the cabins from the pitching and rolling. Winds ran at 39 MPH and gusted to over 50! The tug listed as much as 30 degrees at times. We finally docked the barge in Baltimore Harbor, thank goodness!

"Why do I like this as a vacation? The pace is slow but sure. The details are interesting and nobody is bossing me around. How else could I do as well? I have no social obligation to meet just because

---

31   Tug captain, Chris Lupton

I have spare time. Bed and board are good and the company is congenial. Right now, in my cabin, I have no idea where we are going now or next time, and it makes no difference. How different from practicing medicine!"

From his diary of a long cruise on the Interstate river tug Transporter, April 1979, by Morris A. Robbins, M.D.

Early in my specialty practice a high school classmate lost his entire left arm in a farm accident. He was an avid deer hunter, usually in Maine. As a means of rehabilitating him—-and adding to my own accomplishments—-I joined the physically demanding yearly deer hunt in northern Maine for eight years. This eventually stopped when another hunting buddy died and I was getting a little too old to hack it. While it lasted, it was wonderful annual basic training and physical conditioning. I still miss it.

During this phase of my career my wife and I maintained a small motor boat which provided short periods of recreation on the river and adjacent creeks. We also had a folding two-place kayak which was used at home and on vacations in the Maine woods and the New Jersey shore. I invented a machine to enable me to use the conventional double kayak paddle with one arm.

Captain Morris Robbins and first mate Betty at the helm of their 14- foot open fishing boat, bought from the Sears catalog.

Chapter 14
SEMI RETIREMENT

The by-laws at Zurbrugg force a chief to step down when he passes sixty-five. In December of 1982, at the annual staff meeting, I relinquished the position and was automatically placed on the Senior Staff. Here, a surgeon may keep on operating, but his other responsibilities are lessened. There was still some unfinished business. I continued for another year as Chairman of the Surgical Division and member-at-large of the Executive Committee.

In 1979 I began to develop cataracts. One eye was worse than the other. The only effect on my surgery was some difficulty with depth perception when sewing up layers of tissue. One of my fellow Cooper interns was pioneering in the now common technique of implantation of acrylic artificial lenses in place of the opaque natural ones. I became one of his experimental group of patients. He operated on both eyes over a period of two years. The first operation was not completely successful because the lens shifted around at times, so it was replaced. The result has been excellent thus far, and I can see better that I ever could, even without glasses. As far as vision goes, I still could operate.

Several years ago, I was instrumental in establishing the Department of Occupational Health at Zurbrugg. It was originally called the Industrial Clinic. We succeeded in enrolling around forty local organizations, including police departments and utility companies. We were available twenty-four hours a day, seven days a week, through cooperation with the Emergency Department. New injuries were sent to us and we followed up as necessary, declaring the patients fit to return to work. The Administrator at that time invited me to become the Medical Director but, since this involved general medicine, I declined. For a while I received orthopedic referrals for follow-up care. This became an important part of my office practice. Recently, hospital administration and department personnel have changed several times. As a result, I rarely see a patient from there unless he or she specifically asks for me.

The latest development (1993) is "managed health care" in which insurance companies demand that consultants and specialists be under contract with the hospital, and on the active staff list, in order to participate in patient care. This now has almost killed my hospital-referred practice even though I want to continue working.

Following retirement as Chief, my referral practice slowed down due to retirement or death of physicians of my generation and new affiliations between the younger practitioners. The malpractice insurance premiums were so high that I had to retire completely to escape them or quit operating under general anesthesia to lower them. The latter requirement was impractical and unrealistic, so I decided to leave all the hospitals, but continue my office practice.

Fortunately, fee-for-service consultations for insurance companies and lawyers began to increase. These are usually independent referee or expert witness evaluations which require careful reports. I am not an "insurance doctor" or a lawyer's tool. My role is to tell the truth as I see it. There have been enough regular clinical patients to keep things interesting. It is pleasing to see some patients return after many years' absence.

The ideal role for a surgeon who is slowing down should be teaching. Actually, this does not happen today. There are so many changes taking place in the name of medical progress that the older doctor is on the defensive. As an example, the procedures, appliances and instruments that have carried me through are becoming outdated. The younger generation is trying Some "new" concepts that we abandoned because we found them defective. When I quit operating, I was using state of the art for that decade, but the younger surgeons were introducing the next decade. Had I been younger, I would have taken time off to catch up with them.

We older doctors knew how to keep costs down. We depended more upon our senses and experience and less on high-priced technology, even when it became available. The new sophisticated diagnostic instruments and techniques are fascinating, but I wonder if they really are so necessary to maintain good health and heal the sick. I definitely feel that they are overused, especially for insured patients. The public is not aware that these new tests often are difficult to interpret and are probably' not as accurate as we think they are. They can reveal normal processes that we have not been able to see before, and we may interpret them as abnormal. There is a possibility that future doctors will diagnose and treat primarily by machine rather than by personal touch and intelligence.

Many years ago, the idea was expressed that the ultimate goal of surgery is to eliminate itself—-to avoid the knife. In several surgical fields this concept is working. Urologists do a lot of their work through tubes and flexible catheters, thereby shaving prostates, burning away bladder tumors, draining abscesses, removing stones, dilating constrictions and making diagnoses. General surgeons do similar procedures through scopes to the chest and abdomen. The laser beam evaporates tissue bloodlessly, even inside the eye. Blood vessels can be catheterized and treated by X-ray guidance. Clots can be removed when circulation is threatened or vessels can be dilated for the same reason. Orthopedics, also, is changing with the arthroscope, whereby diagnosis and several operations can be done without wide joint exposure. The period of recovery is markedly shortened this way. Discs are being repaired through scopes by microsurgery. Aging and experienced surgeons are feeling the pinch because these new techniques have to be learned, and the new people already know them. If this trend continues, the community orthopedist will be concentrating on minor and key-hole surgery through tubes illuminated by fiber optics. The number of major open operations could decrease and be done by regional centers where a few super specialists do the work.

At present, some of the most common major orthopedic operations are total joint replacements. These procedures are becoming more universal, easier to perform and presumably less risky. Now, you can get your new hip at home, from your local surgeon. The real danger is replacement when an older procedure would suffice or the patient is so young, heavy or physically active that the endoprosthesis (artificial joint) will not hold up. As I have stated before, the voice of experience is often ignored by new specialists who are anxious to add to their repertoire of skills and financial stabilization. In addition, hospital rules push the elders aside to make room for youngsters with their more profitable procedures.

The professional liability insurance carriers refuse to lower the premiums for the semi-retired surgeon unless he is placed in a restricted, lower task category. He must limit the number of patients he sees weekly. I cannot be involved in patient care more than twenty hours a week! An increasing number of orthopedists, neurosurgeons and obstetricians, being in the highest risk categories, are leaving practice because of the enormous premiums. Either they go into a less expensive field or retire altogether. Contrary to popular opinion, doctors do not quit because they have been sued, but because they cannot afford the protection.

I resigned from Burdette Tomlin and was graciously placed on the Honorary Staff. My name is still on the roster and I receive the usual Staff literature. I did likewise at Kessler, but received no recognition or announcements. Prior to these moves, by several years, I resigned from Burlington County, also unrecognized.

I am now on the Honorary Staff at Zurbrugg and kept informed. Here, I did not resign, but continued to operate until the early '80s. Without consultation or fanfare, I was informed that I was no longer "active," and my privilege sheet came back empty. I still do not know why this happened. Maybe I was not admitting enough patients to satisfy the new administration or was suddenly considered an insurance risk. The Emergency Department is off-limits to me, also.

In mid-1993s after I wrote this chapter, Zurbrugg became the victim of economics, business and politics. It was forced to eliminate most of its acute care beds and limp along with short term emergency care and social service enterprises. The future of my favorite hospital is in doubt.[32]

We took two extensive tours after I left Zurbrugg. The first was in Alaska during the Spring breakup (a mixture of ice and mud in the tundra) I flew to the "top of the world, Point Barrow, about 1200 miles from the North Pole. Alaska is a "must" experience, but no place to live unless one starts when he is still young! The second trip was the Canadian Rockies. This is a place of unsurpassed beauty, considered equal to Switzerland by people who have been to Europe. The walk on a large glacier is unforgettable.

Many people who retire from their primary job hope to spend more time with their families. Actually, the children have matured and moved away. I have more time for home and shop, but recreation has suffered from diminished income. My marine activities have ceased altogether, including vacation stints in the Merchant Marine. My mechanical daydreams are taking shape in models and experiments, but there is little chance of putting them on the market. I love to write~ but have had little luck in getting published.

---

32   Zurbrugg was bought out by another hospital in Willingboro, and then closed.

My wife and I are thankful to be alive, healthy and occupied. We still live in our Delanco home, drive our aging cars and do our own house and yard work. Our kids are successful in their own right. Dorothy works in Washington for the Department of the Treasury and her husband for Census. Bill is an accomplished wood artisan and his wife investigates municipal bonds for insurability, in New York City. There are four granddaughters to date, whom we see too infrequently.

I am not sure how long I can hold out professionally, even if my health continues to be good. At this writing, the government is interfering with, and trying to improve, medical care. We older doctors are pessimistic about the outcome

My office nurse frequently asks me if I am bitter about the way I have been treated. I assure her I am not. My life and career have been successful and happy, and I am widely known and respected, so what could be better?

Recognition of Fifty Years in the Medical Society, May 1995

Chapter 15

RETIREMENT

This account has been written in stages over a period of fifteen years, which accounts for the mixture of past and present tense. I believe it is more pleasant and interesting to read this way, and it reflects my mood at various times in my career.

Morris A. Robbins, M.D.
313 West Broad Street
Burlington, New Jersey 08016
(609) 386-0313

... announces the closing of his orthopedic office on December 31, 1994.

Requests for record transfers should be by mail. Available by telephone Mondays and Wednesdays.

By December, 1994, my office staff and I decided we had had enough rules, regulations, directives and expense. Managed care was closing in on us. An office computer system was becoming mandatory, and we had neither expertise nor money to install one. Furthermore, I had been practicing fifty years. Health was not a problem. We closed the practice on the last day of the year.

> *"...it was exactly fifty years ago that my husband, Arthur Peacock, left his first medical practice here in Columbus – turning it over to a promising young physician known as Morris Robbins. Young Dr. Robbins not only took over the practice – he and his wife Betty bought our comfortable old house on Main Street, as well – and made it their home. I recall so well the evening when we invited all of Arthur's patients to an informal reception to greet*

their new Doctor and his lovely wife – both of whom came from families who were no strangers to the community. Fifty years! So much has happened in that swiftly passing time. Columbus was just the starting point. You moved on into the specialty that had been nearest to your heart – orthopedic surgery – and against many odds, your determination and innate skill took you to the top. Not only have you helped make life better for hundreds of patients, you have also been an inspiration to people like myself, who hold the deepest admiration for your achievements, and your personal character. My husband, Arthur, followed your career with intense interest, and was gratified to see what you made of your life." (Letter from Mary Peacock, widow of Dr. Arthur Peacock, on Morris Robbins' retirement, 1994).

"Congratulations on your retirement. You have earned it. You have had a long and distinguished medical career of over 50 years, starting as a General Practitioner and concluding as an Orthopedic surgeon. We at the medical profession have been blessed with having Morris Robbins as a colleague. But of greater importance is the trust and admiration you have earned from your patients. Those memories will be retained long after awards and other recognition by the profession are forgotten. "(Letter from Dr. Robert Heal upon Doc's retirement*)*

Upon the advice of a colleague who was Medical Director of the Board of Medical Examiners I maintained and renewed my license to practice, just in case I might need it at times. I rarely use it except for giving advice when requested or for appropriate emergencies. My license was valid for six more months. There was so little indication that renewal was advisable that I gave it up. Now it is illegal for me to treat anyone or even give official advice. My medical career is history.

Removable campling trailor for a pick-up; Doc created dozens of 1:12 size wooden models of his inventions. All were designed to allow mobility and independence for victims of paralysis: a wheelchair that climbed stairs, a variety of self-contained vehicles for travel, motorized scooters, and other devices. He never patented any of his inventions, nor did he market nor sell his ideas. Interestingly, some of his designs have now been made by others and are in common use. The models and drawings have been donated to the University of Pennsylvania.

Now, I am reverting to my second career choice of mechanical engineering, as an amateur. My inventions are primarily of biomechanical devices for assisting handicapped people. Also, a life-long interest in transportation machinery occupies some of my time.

Throughout my life, the only time that people have paid any real attention to or used my ideas is during the period when I treated them medically or surgically. People still remind me of what I was fortunate enough to do for them in conventional practice. Over the years I have voluntarily made special braces, artificial limbs and transportation devices for individuals, but in no case that I can recall has anyone ever used them. This has been extremely frustrating, especially since I know first-hand what is desirable and I have the ability to make them. The lame and halt still inspire me to devise mechanical aids for them but the plans and prototypes become part of the archives. I hope to accumulate these products of inspiration into an atlas in the hopes that someone will benefit at some future time.

Retirement has removed the deadlines and constant demands of the past. I can work when I am inspired and feel like it. The property furnishes exercise. Reading used to be confined to medical literature. Now I am reading the classics and reviewing college subjects. My office records are being culled so that only my operations and some other outstanding cases are being saved. All records of the last seven years must be retained for legal reasons.

Thirty-six years of orthopedic office records present an endless opportunity to keep busy. There is hardly any point in composing articles pertaining to my practice because of the rapidly changing nature of the profession. The one thing missing in this situation is an earned income. Since my heyday preceded the inflated fees of today, my wife and I must trim things closely.

By now, the lack of membership credentials means nothing to me, the same as if I had them. After retirement one is no longer considered as a member of the organized medical profession.

Chapter 16
THE CHANGING MEDICAL CLIMATE IN THE LAST HALF CENTURY

During the decade of the '80s the public became disillusioned with the medical profession. Now, consumerism is in vogue. Many patients believe they can plan and control their treatment better than their doctors can, and they act accordingly. When they are frustrated or greedy, they tend to use their doctors as scapegoats, both verbally and legally. Physicians and surgeons, being human, may reciprocate and treat patients at arm's length, expecting them to strike at any time. I understand this same attitude exists in the other professions, services and industry.

Complaining patients seem to think that "all doctors are alike." Recently, many people have told me they "hate doctors." They seem to view all physicians as evil, except the ones who specifically protect them. A doctor has to be extremely effective and convincing today to command respect and keep it.

Doctors are considered to be stereotyped and stencil-duplicated—-stamped out like automobiles. Truthfully, I do not believe the public is entirely wrong. I disagree that medical practitioners are as defective as pictured, but they are coming out very much alike. Medical schools favor outstanding college grades, relatives of alumni, good financial backing and other irrelevant considerations as prerequisites for admission. This undoubtedly stamps graduating medical students as clones. There are families in which it is traditional and mandatory that at least one child becomes a doctor or lawyer. These people usually are city-bred, and they tend to practice in or near the urban areas. Over the years they seem to have monopolized metropolitan and academic medicine. Additionally, there has been a recent influx of foreign medical graduates ·who exhibit first generation immigrant characteristics: hard working, aggressive and business-like. Furthermore, licensing, certifying, registration and practice regulations by government, medical organizations and hospitals exert equalizing pressures upon young doctors. They are forced to act and think alike to survive.

All physicians and surgeons have been scientific since the medical schools were culled and improved after World War I. Premedical education has been primarily scientific and medical courses predominately so. Modern medicine claims to be a science superior to the ancient healing arts. Schools have not taught the art of medicine. This has to be innate or learned from long experience. The typical scientist dislikes the inexactness and emotions of human nature. The new doctor is heavy on knowledge and light on experience. The idea that physicians are impersonal stems from such influences. The modern doctor hardly has time to listen to the patient, even if he wants to. These attributes give patients the impression that doctors are arrogant. In many cases, they are overbearing and intolerant but, unfortunately, so are many patients. In intense situations, two unrelenting forces must clash. To avoid this, one force should submit to the other. In medicine the patient is the pleader and should submit to his doctor for best results.

People are convinced that the modern doctor is greedy. They resent the showcase real estate, expensive automobiles, luxurious vacations, conspicuous recreation and conversations about investments and securities. I don't like this flaunting of affluence, either. On the other hand, people might be jealous of success!

The worst breach in doctor-patient relationship is the view that doctors are stupid or malicious. Stupid people cannot become doctors. Only a criminal doctor would choose to malpractice. Medical mistakes are made because human judgment is involved, but not maliciousness. Education and training do not necessarily improve character, but immoral and unethical people are supposedly rejected before they are turned loose on the public. Discontent and litigation spring from emotional conflicts rather than premeditated wrongdoing on the part of the doctor. They also come from public greed for easy, tax-free cash.

Long term memory has a forgiving element and merciful forgetfulness of the unpleasant events and feelings of the past. History often becomes legend rather than fact. The public may pine for the old-time country doctor whose likeness is no more to be found. Older physicians are equally nostalgic over conditions in the early days of their career, and are glad to have been a part of them. I, too, am glad I am not just starting out, with the knowledge of what has transpired before.

Fifty years ago, the community doctor was considered an honorable, capable, dedicated, educated and reliable man. There were only a few lady doctors then. He was definitely middle class and financially comfortable, but not apt to be rich or flaunt his possessions. He lived in the nice part of town, in a substantial house with office attached, but not in millionaire's row. He drove a middle grade domestic automobile, such as a Buick ("the doctors" car"), but rarely a Cadillac or Lincoln. He wore himself out serving his patients at all hours of the day or night, and was loved for his dedication. There was magic in his treatment room and prescription pad. His presence was noted and respected. Everything was done to help him on his rounds and to avoid interference with his availability. Personally, and socially, but not necessarily financially, he was considered a top man in his community. Many people owed him money[33]. He was usually a general practitioner who delivered the local babies and cared for his patients from cradle to grave. Specialists lived in the cities and were rarely called in.

The small-town doctor did minor, and sometimes major, surgery. There were only a few full-time general surgeons available in the local hospitals. These institutions were basically surgery-oriented. The office shingle and the Caduceus, or green cross, on his license plate were an honor and passport. Everything had a dignity to it. Young people became doctors because they wanted to, and they came from all walks of life. There was no question that it was great to be a doctor!

Lest you think I am dreaming of Utopia, I will admit that I can recall a spectrum of outstanding, average and poor practitioners. But that is the point. Doctors used to be individuals, and often colorful characters as well. People respected them for their differences and gravitated toward the ones they liked. For instance, some were alcoholic, but their devotees insisted they were better when they were half drunk. Some were smooth, genteel and sophisticated; others were rough, vulgar and loud. All were usually capable. Most doctors never attended refresher courses since there were none to speak

---

33   Debt collection was always difficult for Doc, despite the dedication of his small office staff in following through with billing. Years after his death, a former patient was extolling the success Doc had in restoring this man to full functioning. He ended the conversation with, "I guess I should have paid him."

of, but they read, learned from experience, and attended medical society and hospital staff meetings where they exchanged ideas freely.

But the climate has changed. The influx of innumerable young doctors, regimented and intense education, worship of informational knowledge and pressure of hospital residency training programs have altered the picture. Urbanization of the countryside has so changed the scene that the individualistic, dedicated, overworked, colorful, outstanding practitioner has been engulfed and altered in the deluge to the point that he no longer exists or seems desirable. The present generation has little idea what its parents' medical experiences were like.

The public also has changed. Patients used to be loyal to "their doctor" and trusted him. "Whatever you say. You're the doctor!" was a common expression that is rarely heard today. They depended upon him for most of their medical needs, and usually resented being referred elsewhere. In spite of this general trend, there were those who went to a different doctor for each ailment, but these people were not very ill.

Hometown folks did not always trust the local doctor, and some chose a man in the next town. We used to complain that if patients went to the hometown doctor medical practice would be less tiring. In those days we attended over half of our patients in their homes, even for minor ailments. If you were sick enough to lie down the doctor had to come to you. Doctor shopping was a habit of hypochondriacs, deadbeats, transients and the rare drug addict. The new man in town was tested for the more simple ailments ("honeymooned") and by the shoppers. Of course, some patients became dissatisfied and would go so far as to threaten the doctor physically, but they would not sue him. I know whereof I speak.

The average doctor practiced decent medicine out of self-respect and dedication to his patients. He did his best with what he had available, and his patients went along, knowing that results would not always be desirable. They were inclined to resign themselves to God's will, without the intervention of lawyers.

The recent upsurge of litigation has changed the medical climate. At present, every doctor must practice defensive medicine, throwing the whole book at his patient in a sometimes-futile effort to protect himself. He must also satisfy the increasing demands of hospitals, government and insurance companies. The third party is king. No medical record is secret when someone else pays the bill. Therefore, patients' 'records must be complete, noncommittal and written in acceptable language to the courts. Cue comments for private reminder to the doctor are dangerous, as are late or amended entries. Plaintiff's attorneys scrutinize every inch of the chart and folder, so nothing is sacred! Every off-the-cuff or telephone conversation had better be noted because patients' memories are very short in the courtroom.

A large portion of the modern doctor's time is spent examining people, both deserving and dishonest, for the purpose of evaluating disability and compensation. A growing number of people seem to be intent upon obtaining compensation and avoiding work, rather than getting well quickly and making their all-too-short lives productive and memorable. They worship their lawyer and expect the doctor to be a pawn to further their interests.

A half century ago life was simpler and more pleasant. Whether or **not it** was totally better, I am not sure. Young people knew earlier what they wanted to do and were anxious to get going. The Depression made us realize that the world does not owe us a living. Welfare was embarrassing and only a temporary necessity. Ambition was encouraged because the Alternative education, times was a was undesirable. Students were not afraid to work for their and were serious about achieving success. One product of the growing preoccupation with the "buck," but then it was necessary to heal the paralyzed economy. Once established in an occupation, people seemed satisfied with advancement by increments, and they welcomed advice from their elders and superiors. A larger percentage of young doctors sprang from the soil and nonmedical families **than** today. Most recruits looked upon medicine as a calling, similar to the ministry. The physician, like the clergy, was born and trained to be apart, and he expected honor from his flock. He was apt to live up to his part of the bargain. Naturally, this was my model. Things began to change after World War II. Eager young doctors became interested in the specialties as a result of their experiences with combat injuries. A good example is orthopedic surgery. Most of the military doctors were discharged in a short span of time. They were accustomed to hospital-based specialty practice rather than general medicine. As a result, they sought specialty training and certification before settling down to private practice. The general practitioner pool shrank.

Workmen's' Compensation gradually changed public attitude from self-sufficiency to dependency and habituation. Today, thousands of people are addicted to the tax-free benefits of temporary, partial permanent, or permanent disability. They pride themselves on the discovery that they may make more money from disability than by working. Even more reprehensible, I believe, is a new, but small, breed of money-hungry doctors who profit from prolonging the disability period with excessive or unnecessary treatments. Welfare has definitely become a way of life for inadequate personalities. Succeeding generations from the same family feed from the public trough, even when they fail to show objective signs that they are physically unfit to work. They panhandle from the government and insurance companies rather than on the street.

Although World War II was over decades ago, the specialty trend continues. Many of today's doctors were not born then. The rise of medical insurance plans and general affluence has made medical practice highly remunerative and desirable as a livelihood. Competition has become intense. Too many doctors are crowding into the same community. Cut-throat tactics, brazen advertising and commercialism are the inevitable result, in contrast to the dignified, uncontested professionalism of the past. Competition breeds excessive tests, drug therapy, physical therapy and surgery, both for economic and legal self-defense—-and greed. Medicolegal defensive tactics are extremely expensive.

Medical care has always been available at some level for those who seek it. We used to treat the poor for nothing or barter. The hospital free clinics were available, with all specialties represented. Poor patients were referred by local physicians and were screened by social service workers. Necessary hospitalization was included. The county or some local agency paid the hospital, at cost, and the patients gradually reimbursed the agency if they could. Poor people usually make poor patients. Clinics, recognizing this, became expert at handling such people and encouraging them to cooperate in their own care. One of the inviolable prerequisites for hospital staff privileges for all doctors, except consultants, was free service in the clinics of their specialty. This service included inpatients referred from the clinic. There was admittedly a two-tier medical system, but it was available and effective for those who actively sought aid.

Now that national medical plans are being hotly discussed, let me propose a return of the erstwhile principle of the hospital free clinics. Let the government, probably through the Public Health Service, establish dispensaries throughout communities and 'pay salaries to local physicians, nurses and ancillary workers to man them on a part-time basis.[34] Have the services available daily. Screen the population so that only the deserving people may use the service at times when they are financially unable to pay for their care. Pay the hospitals for inpatients referred by the dispensaries at cost. Simplify the system by shelling out money as it is needed, rather than for future necessity by vouchers and insurance schemes. This method should relieve hospital emergency departments of nonemergency visits. Eliminate Medicaid entirely, with its expensive, complicated, time-consuming details. An alternative plan would be to keep Medicaid and let it pay for the clinics. To add to the intensified situation, para- and quasi-medical professions have inserted themselves into the traditional territory of the M.D. Years ago, homeopaths were accepted by allopaths as equals.

Another system, osteopathy, is being incorporated into conventional medical practice, although it still maintains its own schools and associations. Therapeutic manipulation is still part of their regimen. The sudden sprint of podiatry, formerly chiropody, is more controversial. They definitely have their place in office practice, as "foot doctors," and in hospital for the supplemental care of feet, especially in diabetics. Now they represent themselves as orthopedic surgeons specializing in lower extremities. In my opinion, they are not yet qualified for their desired position.

The most recent contenders are the chiropractors. Fundamentally, chiropractic is based on principles that are unacceptable to conventional doctors. As physical therapists they are valuable, but their diagnoses lack credibility for the rest of us. Their "medicine" is vitamins, minerals and natural foods. Their tests are noninvasive and often exaggerated in their importance or diagnostic value. Future success depends upon public acceptance and pressure on the hospitals. Third parties increasingly recognize them.

In all fairness to modern medicine, it is usually able to cure disease through scientific diagnosis and treatment. It is horribly expensive and rather impersonal. The new government concept of "the health care industry" is insulting to older practitioners, and is proving to be fatal to true

---

34   Doc submitted his proposals to Sen. William Bradley, who was working on legislative changes to the medical care system, and to President Ford. His contributions were acknowledged by both.

dedication, thoughtfulness and professionalism. Older patients do not like this trend, either.

In spite of government control and liberal philosophy, the two-tier system still prevails as far as utilization is concerned. In isolated rural areas the general practitioner is still king. In remote or economically devastated areas it is impossible for a doctor to survive. Near the larger urban areas, it is not realistic to maintain that all patients are, or wish to be, treated alike. People on welfare still tend to be difficult to handle and careless about their health. They do not have the erstwhile "mother hens" to keep them in the mainstream of modern medicine, where the government is trying to put them.

In 1992, government and business seriously intruded in the doctors' private offices. Medicare, followed by private insurance, initiated a reform of reporting, billing and reimbursement. To standardize procedure, a system of coding was started for each diagnosis and procedure. This was obviously designed to aid the clerks in the insurance offices to know what buttons to push on the computer. It actually complicated things so badly 'that everyone is confused, doctors and suppliers are not being paid properly and patients are not being reimbursed. Busy practices must hire clerks just to fill out forms, thereby increasing overhead. The third parties are now actually attempting to control medical practice by telling the doctor what he is allowed to do, and in what order! If this becomes standard procedure the doctor will be a mere technician obeying nonmedical bosses. The invaluable asset of educated, reasonable, professional judgment will be sacrificed.

A second serious assault and insult is intrusion of the Occupational Safety and Health Administration (OSHA). It is mandating actual office procedure on a standardized basis regardless of size or type of practice. Not only does it control disposition of used disposable equipment, such as syringes, needles, swabs and dressings, but it has strict rules for personnel clothing and office laundry. Hired inspectors are supposed to invade the office and the doctors must pay them to come. Registered disposal services must remove waste for a price. The threat of overwhelming fines for any breaking of the rules is emphasized.

These two predicaments present solo practitioners and any office with a limited practice, especially in terms of income, with the almost inevitable decision to call it quits! I know of no available insurance protection against this situation, and wonder if the public would intervene to save their doctors if they realize what is going on.

Rest assured. There still are good, dedicated, knowledgeable, effective and efficient doctors available almost everywhere. Again, it is a matter of individuality. One cannot completely rely on credentials, location, position, published articles, advertising, publicity or other artifacts to find a good doctor. There are still many deserving students who make it and stay clean. Furthermore, good doctors improve with experience, but poor ones remain that way. If you believe you have a good one, be thankful and stay with him or her. Hope that the time will never come when you have no choice!

THE END

EPILOGUE

Thursday, September 16, 2004

Paid

MORRIS ALLEN ROBBINS, M.D.

Morris Allen Robbins, M.D. on September 15, 2004 of Delanco, NJ at home. Age 87 years.

Beloved husband for 59 years of Elizabeth nee Sutton Robbins, and father of Dorothy and husband Jose Talavera, Riverton, NJ, William M. and wife Karen Robbins, Vincentown, NJ. Also his grandchildren Sarah Robbins, Nancy Talavera, Elizabeth Talavera, Emily Talavera and niece Lorraine Woods, Hamilton Twp., NJ, nephews Lynn Croshaw, Florence S.C., John Parkes, Florence, NJ.

Dr. Robbins was born and raised in Jacksonville, and graduated from Mt. Holly High School Class of 1934. He was a graduate of University of Pennsylvania Class 1941, University of Maryland, Baltimore Campus, The graduate School of Medicine University of Pennsylvania. He completed a pre-ceptorate of Orthodpedic Surgery under Dr. Vernon Davis. He was a member of the Burlington County Medical Association and practiced Medicine for 50 years. He was on the staff of Mt. Holly Hospital, Cooper Hospital Camden, Kessler Memorial Hospital Hammonton, Zurbrugg Memorial Hospital Riverside, Burdette Tomlin Hospital Cape May Court House, NJ. He was a past president of the Burlington County Medical Society and was a former Chief of Orthopedic Surgery at Zurbrugg Memorial Hospital Riverside and Kessler Memorial Hospital Hammonton.

Funeral services will be held 11 AM Monday at the Beverly Presbyterian Church, Warren St., Beverly, NJ. Interment Cedar Hill Cemetery, Florence, NJ. Friends may call at the church from 9:30 until service time at 11 AM. Contributions may be made to the Phillip Mann Challenge Fund C/O Bev-erly Presbyterian Church, War-ren Street, Beverly, NJ.

Arrangements by McGEE FUNERAL HOME, 869 Beverly Road, Burlington, NJ.

In September 2020 Doc's papers, scale models of his inventions and protheses were donated to his alma mater, The University of Pennsylvania. University President Amy Gutman wrote, *"Your father sounds like a model of resilience and ingenuity, and I greatly enjoyed learning about the life and career of such a remarkable Penn alumnus."*

Morris A. Robbins, '44
Delanco, N.J.
September 16, 2004

At the age of 18, Dr. Robbins lost his
left forearm and half of his right hand in
an electrical accident, but he was determined to overcome his disability. Upon
completion of his medical degree, he
received training at Maryland and The
Cooper Hospital in Camden, N.J. He
operated a general practice in Columbus from 1945 to 1954. In 1956, he
attended graduate school at the University of Pennsylvania and accepted an
orthopaedic preceptorship in Camden
from 1957 to 1960. Dr. Robbins was
chief orthopaedic surgeon at Burdette
Tomlin Memorial Hospital in Cape
May and at Zurbrugg Memorial
Hospital in Riverside; he also operated
a private orthopaedic surgery practice
from 1960 until retirement in 1994.
He is survived by wife Betty, daughter
Dorothy, son William and four grandchildren.

"In Memorium" section of the alumni Bulletin magazine of the Medical Alumni
Association of the University of Maryland

"A thank you note here: Thank you for what you did back in 1963
when I showed up in your office as a fourteen year- old with a
slipped epiphysis. Because of what you did in the series of oper-
ations subsequently performed, I was able to finish college and
go on into a career in aviation after a bit of graduate school. I'm
happy to report that I have successfully completed my final flight
at American Airlines and have retired (mandatory at age 60)."
(Letter from former patient Ted Fergus to Dr. Robbins, Mar.
10, 2008; Captain Fergus did not know that Doc had died, and
was grieved to learn the news.)

Morris A. Robbins, M.D.

A Most Uncommon Gentleman

With a most uncommon intellect,
He cracked the codes of medicine,
His chosen vocation ,
Defying, courageously, all odds and obstacles
To heal all whom he touched.

With a most uncommon compassion,
He connected with all peoples,
 Leading with conviction,
But with such gentleness and generosity,
To embrace all whom he touched.

With a most uncommon style,
He set his own standards,
From T-bird to driving 'cap'
Sporting those 'natty' vests,
To charm all whom he touched.

And with a most uncommon abiding love,
He played his part in all of our lives,
Sharing his extraordinary gifts,
To enrich all whom he touched.

We are so abundantly thankful for such
Intellect, such compassion, such style,
And above all,
For such extraordinary abiding love.

He will forever dwell in our hearts
As the Most Uncommon of Gentleman!

For Mrs. Robbins and Family

With Love from,
        Timothy

Christmas 2004

Tribute by family friend Timothy Horan; reprinted with permission from
the author

The Delanco Historical Commission added Doc's biography to their website in the section called "Key Figures in Delanco History".

delancotownship.com
· Key Figure in Delanco History
·· **Morris A. Robbins, MD** (1917-2004): Morris A. Robbins was born on a farm in Springfield, the son of Clarence R. Robbins, a carpenter, and Sarah Poinsett Robbins, a teacher. He was raised in Jacksonville, NJ, where he was active in the YMCA. At the age of 19, Robbins lost his left forearm and half of his right hand and was burned severely over most of his body in a tragic electrical accident. In spite of this handicap, he was determined to overcome his disability. Robbins graduated from the University of Pennsylvania and the University of Maryland Medical School in 1944. Upon completion of his medical degree, he trained at Maryland and Cooper Hospital in Camden, N.J. He operated a general practice in Columbus from 1945 to 1954. In 1956, Dr. Robbins moved his family to 1410 Second Street near the corner of Peachtree Avenue in Delanco. He attended graduate school at the University of Pennsylvania and accepted an orthopedic preceptorship in Camden from 1957 to 1960. Dr. Robbins performed his medical practice over more than 50 years. He served as chief orthopedic surgeon at Burdette Tomlin Memorial Hospital in Cape May Court House and Zurbrugg Memorial Hospital in Riverside; he also practiced at Kessler Memorial Hospital in Hammonton, and operated a private orthopedic surgery practice in Burlington from 1960 until retirement in 1994. He was president of the Burlington County Medical Society. In his rare spare time, Dr. Robbins was an inventor and essayist. Doc, as most people called him, was known around town for the vehicles he drove: a 1956 Thunderbird, an aging Ford Bronco, and a tricycle. Dr. Robbins died in 2004, survived by his wife Betty, daughter Dorothy Robbins-Talavera, son William, and four grandchildren.

Former patient Edward Hartmann of Riverton, New Jersey, painted this portrait of Doc in the artist's "NJ Heroes" collection, based on a photograph that appeared in the December 19, 1994 <u>Burlington County Times</u>.

May 2010   BEVERLY BEE   Page 7

By Delanco Township

Delanco

ynship Award Events

Mayor of Delanco, Kate Fitzpatrick, presents a proclamation to Mrs. Betty Robbins honoring her husband Dr. Morris Robbins, an accomplished orthopedic surgeon who died in 2004. Delanco officials passed an ordinance naming a proposed street after the long time resident of Delanco that will now be known as Robbins Lane

NANCY ROKOS / STAFF PHOTOGRAPHER

An **unnamed road** in Delanco that extends from Magnolia Lane past Second Street to the riverbank has been named Robbins Lane after the late Dr. Morris A. Robbins, who died in 2004.

Delanco honors late Dr. Morris A. Robbins

A previously unnamed road now bears his name.

By Kristen Coppock
Staff writer

kcoppock@phillyBurbs.com
609-871-8073

DELANCO — An inspirational doctor who struggled against adversity has been immortalized with his own street name.

During Monday night's Township Council meeting, officials passed an ordinance naming Robbins Lane after the late Dr. Morris A. Robbins, who died in 2004.

The previously unnamed road extends from Magnolia Lane past Second Street to the riverbank. Township officials said the 50-foot-wide, 411-foot-long stretch is commonly known to residents as Glitters Gulch. A sign will be posted to mark the new designation.

Robbins lived in the township for more than 50 years with his wife, Betty, according to Deputy Mayor Joan Hinkle, a longtime neighbor of the family. He was an accomplished orthopedic surgeon, despite having only one arm, and created his own prosthetics.

The council also presented Robbins' family with a plaque and a proclamation honoring his career and accomplishments. The proclamation calls him "a great surgeon" and "an extraordinary gentleman."

Betty Robbins, 91, attended the presentation with the couple's children, Dorothy Talavera of Delanco and Bill Robbins of Southampton, and their spouses, as well as the couple's grandchildren and great-grandchild.

In 1990, Robbins told a Burlington County Times reporter that he lost his hand in 1935 at age 18 after coming to the aid of a car accident victim. He tripped over a 33,000-volt bare wire that was down in rain-slicked grass on the side of the road. Robbins was electrocuted and lying on the wire when a man pushed him off with a stick. His left arm was severely burned and had to be amputated.

According to the 1990 story, Robbins was taken to Burlington County Hospital in Mount Holly and remained hospitalized for three years. Inspired by the medical staff that treated him, he decided to become a doctor. Despite concerns about his disability, Robbins proved the naysayers wrong. He became an orthopedic surgeon with a private practice in Burlington City.

After creating a homemade prosthesis out of wood, Robbins eventually was accepted at the University of Maryland. Throughout his life, he experimented with materials to create different prosthetics, including some with moving parts that offered dexterity.

His story became a source of inspiration to countless people who knew him. Granddaughter Liz Burmeister of Bordentown City said the doctor was rejected by medical schools because of his disability.

"We miss him terribly," Burmeister said after the presentation.

Hinkle was instrumental in creating the honor for Robbins. She said every street ending at the river has a bench except for the lane.

Hinkle was contacted by Talavera regarding the parklike setting at the end of the road and proposed formally establish-

125

DOC'S FAMILY

Portrait of Doc and Betty in 1997 by Torre Studios,
Burlington, New Jersey

Elizabeth (Betty) Robbins was Doc's left hand. Literally. He made a mold of her hand to construct articulated fingers for his prothesis that would fit in a surgical glove. Before marriage, Betty earned degrees from the Women's College of North Carolina and Drexel University. She managed food and nutrition at the first Devereaux camp for developmentally challenged children, ran the nursery of a women's prison, and was the dietician and home economics teacher for a girls' boarding school in El Paso, Texas. Teaching again entered her life when it was her turn to support the family. She was known as an excellent hostess. She was active in her church and community, particularly in the Medical Society Auxiliary and Zurbrugg Hospital Auxiliary. Betty's quiet, efficient, behind-the-scenes management of the home and their active social life made it possible for Doc to have the career he did. She died in 2011.

Dot and Doc

Dorothy Robbins Talavera started her career at the White House in Washington, DC. She became a professional in-service training developer and manager, ending up at the Bureau of Alcohol, Tobacco and Firearms. Upon being eligible for early retirement, she and her family moved back home to Burlington County, where she started a second career as a high school Spanish teacher. Now working on Act Three, Dorothy is documenting family history, taking advantage of the wealth of primary source materials in the family archives. She has two books to her credit, as well as a long list of published articles.

Bill and wife Karen Robbins at Bifocal Farm

William (Bill) Robbins' pursuit of his professional degrees led him to West Virginia and Tennessee. He has followed his dream by building a career in woodworking and animal husbandry, interests he developed at the feet of his two grandfathers. He is acclaimed for his conservation of historic Quaker meetinghouse furniture, as well as his volunteer restoration work on the oyster schooner A. J. Meerwald. On his Vincentown, NJ Bifocal Farm, he raises lambs and makes fine custom furniture sold through galleries and fine art catalogues. He has been featured numerous times in the press. His work can be seen at www.williamrobbinsfurniture.com and Instagram.

APPENDIX

DEC 19 1990

Special man became surgeon his way

Jack Knarr

Dr. Morris Robbins sat in his warm office in Burlington the other day and told the most harrowing story you'll ever want to hear. It makes you cringe.

It was 1935. Robbins was 18 and driving in his Erskine when he came upon a car accident.

"In those days there weren't any emergency squads," he said, "and the law said you had to stop for accidents and help the people.

"Anyhow, all of what happened is what they tell me happened — hearsay — because the jolt knocked the bleep out of me for 12 hours."

"I got out of the left side of my car, came around the back of my car, and went over to the accident," Robbins said. "And when we got done, I walked around the front of the car, and I tripped over this 33,000-volt bare wire laying in the grass.

And it was raining and the grass was about a foot high."

Imagine every electric-chair horror story. The voltage gripped the boy, wouldn't let him go.

"I was laying right over the wire," Robbins said. "Some soldier came along and found a board and a stick — he stood on the board, and knocked me off the wire with the stick."

What courage. But Robbins was unconscious and horribly burned. He was taken to then-Burlington County Hospital in Mount Holly.

"I woke up in a white tent in bed," he said. "It was a heat tent. I was naked except for something over my crotch, laying there in that thing.

"And I looked around and saw my left arm burned and scarred black. I could see bones and no muscle, nerves laying out there in the open. Every time somebody would touch one of those nerves, I'd jump."

They loaded him up with morphine. Both hands were burned, both sides, his belly and his chin.

"I knew they were going to have to amputate. They didn't have to tell me," he said. "There was no meat there, just bone, and that nerve. And the hand was black.

"So they finally did a 'guillotine amputation,' sawed the bones off straight like that," he said. "Later they reamputated to make a round stump."

All the while, they worked to save Robbins' blackened and deformed right hand.

"In those days they took island grafts. They'd take a needle and pick up a 'tent' of skin, and cut under it, and that would be the whole layer of skin. And then they would 'plant' them like islands (on the wound)," he said. "And new skin would grow out from those islands."

Robbins showed the top of his right hand, which remains all curved, fingers clawed and strong.

"You can almost see them yet. Here's one right here." He showed an island-like scar.

Please see KNARR/C5

129

A special man became surgeon despite handicap

DEC 19 1990

■ KNARR/From A1

That hand gradually healed. With it, Robbins began constructing artifical left arms to wear.

And all through his life, he has improved the models. I wish you could actually touch his "wooden" arm — the complicated mass of maple and fiberglass pieces, Dacron, polyethylene, Teflon, and rubber bands that he has created to serve as his "missing" arm.

The other day, the good doctor was kind enough to unbutton his sleeve and roll it up past the sheath and the elbow. Laced throughout the prosthesis were dozens of rubber bands, knotted and stretched like muscles of the arm, to bound and rebound, doing the work of muscles.

The arm extends and the wooden pieces of the "hand" open and grasp. Robbins must only tighten up or loosen certain arm and shoulder muscles to operate it.

"It's all figured out geometrically, and anatomically," he said.

Robbins wanted to be a doctor, but at Penn he studied zoology. That would be a good backup, while

he found out what he could do. And he put himself to the test.

"The courses I took in college, I took the most meticulous dissecting and microscopic courses I could get," he said. "And I found out I could do it."

Then came what his secretary, Marge Pica, and nurse Tillie Porter call "the miracle." He hoped to go to the University of Virginia. And on the way south, he and a pal got stuck in traffic in Baltimore.

"I looked up, and there was the medical school of the University of Maryland," Robbins said. "I said, 'Dave, stop this car.' I got out and I went in there.

"I fumbled around and I found a back elevator," he said. "There was a sign on there, 'Students not allowed to use this elevator.' Well, I wasn't a student. But I couldn't get the damned thing to run.

"So this bald-headed man comes along, says, 'Can I help you?' I said, 'Yeah, I want to go up to the dean's office.' He said, 'All right, let's go.'

"He goes up, puts me in the dean's office, and goes around the other side of the desk and said, 'What can I do for you?'

"In 15 minutes, I was accepted — without any papers," Robbins said.

The dean saw the homemade prosthesis, along with Robbins'

creativity and determination. He never became a doctor. But when didn't even ask how a man with the receptionist announced that a hands like that could become a doctor. He knew he'd find a way.

"He said, 'There's a place for you in medicine. You're in'." Robbins said.

Robbins had to learn surgery his own way. Then after graduation, he stopped in at Cooper Hospital in Camden to see Dr. Benjamin Franklin Busby, the man who had labored so long and hard over his burned hands.

After the tragedy, Dr. Busby had kindly told Robbins that he could

Dr. Morris Robbins was there, Dr. Busby exclaimed, "Doctor Robbins!" and rushed out in amazement.

That day, Morris was given an internship, and he since has had a long and successful career as a general practitioner in Columbus and an orthopedic surgeon at several hospitals in New Jersey. He's been at 313 W. Broad St. in Burlington since 1960. Only the rare patient would not accept his miracle hands.

BCT staff photo/Rose Shiek

Dr. Morris Robbins shows the artificial arm that helps him perform medical duties.

Robbins and the former Bett Sutton of Florence raised two children, William, 40, and Dorothy Ta lavera, 41.

And he thanks religion for get ting him through those early han times.

"That saved my ass," he sai "When I found out I kept on livin I figured, 'I'm here for somethin I've got to do it'."

He chuckled. "I've been cured since then."

Jack Knarr's human interest column a pears in the Burlington County Times for days each week.

Editorial

The Surgeon's Prosthesis

The evolution of prosthetic hands and arms has been sluggish compared with that of other technology. Utility hooks and simple grasping hands have been improved only slightly over the years. With the advent of plastics, sockets, once made of leather or wood, have become more durable, comfortable, and lightweight, and easier to repair, construct, and fit. The body-powered suspension and control harness has not changed except for the substitution of synthetics for the leather and canvas, which has made it less irritating and malodorous. Specialty end devices are now available for patients who work in some manual occupations. However, there are many types of work in which the person who has a unilateral partial amputation of the arm is not aided by current prostheses because the devices cannot provide enough dexterity, sanitation is inadequate, and the prostheses are incompatible with fluids. One example is surgery.

Just after high-school graduation in 1935, my left arm was amputated below the elbow. I was determined to become an orthopaedic surgeon, but the only way to achieve this goal was to invent and build my own prostheses specifically designed for surgical scrubbing and practical functioning inside the gown and glove. My amputation was on the non-dominant side, so dexterity with instruments such as retractors, hemostats, probes, needle-holders, power drills, and saws was the major requirement.

During the last decade, after I retired from orthopaedic surgery, global research and development in the field of prostheses have concentrated on myoelectrically controlled mechanical hands. Electrical potentials are picked up from the stump and transferred into battery-powered electrical energy that activates motors in the prosthesis. These devices still are totally unsuited for use by a surgeon while operating. They are much too complicated, expensive, and prone to malfunction, and they cannot be surgically scrubbed. Also, their action is too deliberate and slow for some of the movements demanded by operative procedures.

A basic development in my own engineering was the placement of all motor and connecting parts on the surface of the arm socket and hand, thereby eliminating enclosures that could not be scrubbed and dried. Oil or grease lubrication was no longer required. All of my devices have been of the voluntary-opening, automatic-closing type. Ordinary rubber bands attached over the wrist to the hand by braided fishing line and anchored to the proximal edge of the socket by hooks have been an adequate power source. These are scrubbed the same as normal skin, are easily replaced or adjusted, and cannot poke through the sleeve of the gown. The lines are attached to the thumb and fingers, and the tension holds the rotatable hand against the forearm while restraining by friction unwanted supination or pronation. End devices are changed by simply releasing the old bands at the hooks and attaching new ones.

The standard suspension harness was discarded in favor of a single heavy-braided nylon cord tied to the olecranon edge of the socket, looped in figure-of-eight fashion around the scapular region, and enclosing the proximal part of the normal arm as an extensor power source. The other end of the cord extends along the surface of the socket and is attached to the extensor controls of the hand with the use of a safety-pin type of release hook designed for fishing tackle. Shrugging the shoulders opens the fingers and snugs the prosthesis against the stump.

Years ago, I molded the socket around the olecranon and humeral condyles with a cut-out on the volar surface for the bulge of the biceps tendon. This feature has appeared in some current products.

Although the standard voluntary-opening hook is helpful in surgery, if the empty fingers of the glove are inverted, the hook cannot hold metal instruments securely because of the lack of auxiliary supporting surfaces.

Conventional mechanical hands are only a little better than the hook for holding instruments. Any limited-motion hand prosthesis should have the four fingers curved slightly into flexion, the Bunnell position of function, to prevent objects held across the palm from slipping out. I found that by exaggerating the position of function progressively toward the little finger, thus creating two v-shaped niches at the bases of the long, ring, and little fingers, the hand could enter a deeper space and instruments could be held securely at varying angles across the palm, by flexion of the thumb. The simplest construction is a solid wooden or plastic hand that moves only at the metacarpophalangeal joint of the thumb. I have tried joints in the ring and little fingers, but the added complexity offers little practical advantage.

The addition of a joint at the base of the index finger, acting perpendicularly to the thumb joint with cord control for abduction and adduction, increases the number of positions in which instruments can be held by creating the mechanical three-jawed chuck.

1764

Broad (across-the-palm) grip can be improved by the addition of an interphalangeal joint to the thumb. A single extensor cord that crosses the joint and inserts into the dorsum of the distal segment opens the whole thumb, if extension of the new joint is limited to 180 degrees. Two flexor cords are required. One activates the proximal segment and the other, the distal one. The thumb can then curl around an instrument handle, adding security. The tension on the proximal segment should be higher than that on the distal one to prevent the tip of the thumb from touching the apposing finger prematurely during flexion. This precaution preserves pinch grip for flat objects, such as paper or bandage.

In addition to superiority in surgery, my prostheses are at least equal in utility to any on the market, and they do not require gloves for protection or appearance. Because they are flesh-colored, they are neither objectionable nor more noticeable than any other upper-limb prosthesis. Furthermore, they look functional.

I wish these ideas to be in the public domain. The prosthesis industry is encouraged to use them.

Morris A. Robbins, M.D.

Reprinted with permission: Morris A. Robbins, M.D.; "The Surgeon's Prothesis", The Journal of Bone and Joint Surgery, Vol. 76-A, NO. 12, December 1994, pages 1764-1765. https://journals.lww.com/jbjsjournal/ Citation/1994/12000/The_surgeon_s_prosthesis_.2.aspx

WORDS FOR KIDS

TO TEACH WRITING AND READING

by

Morris A. Robbins, MD

First Edition December 2000

*To Emily, From Grandma + Grandpa
Merry Christmas!*

In retirement Doc acquired a word processor, followed by a Mac computer. For the first time he was able to compose, edit, and print his thoughts, using one finger. Prior to that, he dictated his professional correspondence on a Dictaphone for a typist, and wrote his essays and ideas longhand.

Over a period of years, he wrote The Life and Times of a One-Armed Surgeon. He wrote philosophical essays, his thoughts on changes in the medical profession, and specifications of his inventions. Many times, he gave collections of his writings, in three-ring binders, to family and friends as gifts. As he stated, "I love to write." For his grandchildren, he wrote simple explanations and workbooks to help them with their math, grammar, and reading. One of his great talents had always been taking complicated things, and describing them in simple terms, often using analogies.

The Way it Seems to Me
- Short Philosophical Essays on Humanity

Theosophical Essays

Words for Kids to Teach Reading and Writing, 2001,
- developed by Doc to help a learning-disabled granddaughter

Body English, 1995
- A description of common muscles, joint and bone diseases and injuries (orthopedics) in terms a patient can understand

Objective Engineering Essays

Notable Patients, Including Operative and Non-operative

Full Size Prototypes
- Mechanical devices actually tested

Architectural Essays

Physics of Automobile Driving

The Bible Student
- A regular magazine Doc wrote, edited, printed, and distributed through his high school and college years

Introduction

Asked to speak and answer questions.

Title thought up by women - back is clothes-horse and usually aches at some time or other.

Men have this problem too. ♂ aunt reason, ♀ it is natural, you are supposed to know why.

Any back disorder usually → pain in back or legs. We are all familiar ≡ back pain after childhood.

WHAT IS THE BACK?

The <u>foundation</u> of the musculoskeletal system. The backbone is the KEEL. The most powerful groups of muscles lie there or attach to it. A chassis is necessary for land/air animals. Not necessary in water animals except for fast swimmers (muscle levers).

All other structures and organs of the mammalian body are attached to the back. (Stick figure # 1)

All physical forces of the body affect the back - Examples.

Flexible foundation for the head and limbs (24 joints)

Insight into reason for backache and injury being so prevalent.

Embryology. The first structure to appear.

"Navel in the orange" differentiates into 3 layers. (Fig. 2)

Ectoderm → skin, nerves, brain. Stimulus to skin, sent along nerves to spinal cord and brain, processed into action through the motor nerves → response to stimuli. (Beautiful by design?)

Mesoderm → muscles, bones, tubular structure of the blood vessels and heart.

Endoderm → lining for internal organs and blood vessels, heart, lungs, etc.

Neural cleft forms (ditch) - Mesoderm loops around the cleft backwards and forwards. Rear loop becomes the back, Forward loop becomes the abdomen and thorax.

In the centre of the embryonic disc the infalling meets in the middle and forms a neural tube. Ectoderm burys down into the mass of the mesoderm to form the brain, spinal cord and nerve trunks.

the mesoderm thickens and encases the ectodermal canal in tissue which becomes muscles and bone.

The cover-over process continues fore and aft and the neural tube becomes more like a culvert.

Eventually the whole active plate of tissue becomes oval-shaped and starts on its way to become the fetus.

The embryo is also divided into transverse segments or somites. There are 34 segments to begin with.

Each somite growns in its own predestined manner in cooperation with its neighbors to form individual systems of bone, muscle, nerves and blood vessels which mature into the individual vertebrae, muscles and nerve roots and trunks.

In all mammals 3 of these segments at each end pair off and form the individual limbs. These limbs grow out from the sides of the trunk as buds. As they develop they carry along the muscles, nerves and blood vessels which differentiate into the arms and legs. This explains the complexity of the nervous system in the arms and legs. and the charactistic symptoms of disease of any individual segment of the body.

All mammals start out alike, in that the four extremities grow from the side of the body and away from the back toward the belly. They grow at right angles to the back like the four legs of a table. Babies are born with their arms and legs in front of them and it takes them a few weeks to stretch out into the familiar human position. It helps to think of the baby and the four-legged animal in similar terms. (sound?)

When the limbs start to parallel the back bone the limbs (somites) bend where they leave the trunk, but the structures are the same as they were at birth, and continue to be in the four-legged animal.

This explains why back problems affect the arms and legs.

Now confine our thoughts to the back itself and its individual parts.

The early embryonic back consists of a soft, continuous rod in the mesodermal layer from the neck to the tail. When the somites form this notochord remains as a flexible connecting link between the segments. The majority of the width of each somite changes into bone which at first becomes the body of each vertebra. The remaining soft slices of notochord between the vertebral bodies become the intervertebral discs. The core of the notochord stays semi-fluid, much like bleu cheese and remains that way through middle age. The walls of the discs toughen up into round ligaments which bind the adjacent vertebral bodies together along the rim of the bodies. The front (belly side) of the rims, or annular ligaments, are tougher and thicker than they are in the back, so that the softer material in the middle is a little bit off-center.

The development of the vertebra goes on in a backward manner to form a ring which completely encloses the spinal cord, for protection. As the bodies are bound together c̄ flexible discs, the rings or arches, are likewise bound together with a flexible yellow ligament, the ligamentum flavum. This makes a smooth, continuous tube from one end of the spine to the other. Between each arch is a port hole, or neural foramen, through which a branch from the spinal cord emerges, one on each side, at each disc level.

Furthermore, there are levers formed around the rim of the arch, and attached to the arch, which become the insertions for many short muscles, individually about the size of cigarettes. These muscles are laid along

4

the sides of the vertebral bodies and along the back part of them, completely surrounding the arches except where the vertebral bodies are.

There is one more structure which forms between the adjacent vertebral arches. These are the apophyseal joints, which are regular joints similar in size and action to the finger and toe joints. These are placed in such a way that the surface of half of the joint slides on the other, allowing a telescoping action between the arches.

Finally, there are ligaments connecting the levers, or processes. The spinous processes are the bumps or projections along the back. These ligaments are semi-flexible, also. In the thoracic spine there are cross ligaments to the ribs, and in the lower spine there are also ligaments which connect the spine to the pelvis, for stability.

5 There are no muscles along the front of the spine, next to the abdomen. Flexor muscles are placed far outboard along the abdominal wall and the chest wall, to enclose the remainder of the trunk. These muscles are all long and thin, with a much greater degree of contraction per muscle than the shorter muscles in the back. All the organs of the chest and abdomen are enclosed by these trunk muscles.

I have not mentioned the blood vessels of the back. Irrelevant to back pain.

In all mammals the backbone is both a unit and a flexible support column. We all remember, as kids, how flexible our bodies were. The short back muscles must be strong, durable, not easily fatigued, multitudinous in number and direction, to fight off gravity and to position the spine as required at the moment.

138

The shoulder and buttock muscles are also attached to the spinal column to keep the musculo-skeletal system intact. The long, thin, strap-like abdominal muscles must keep active to keep the abdominal contents stable and to allow changes necessitated by breathing and intestinal action. As far as locomotion is concerned, these muscles are quick, short acting, highly contractile and easily fatigued. This is especially noted when the dog, cat or horse gallops along. These muscles snap the front and back legs toward each other, while the shorter muscles in the back maintain position, balance and act in steering. In man, the short back muscles maintain the erect posture, while the abdominal and thoracic muscles take care of forward bending. The back is therefore much stronger than the front is.

The flexibility of the spine is possible only at the discs, the ligamentum flavum, the interspinous ligaments and the apophyseal joints. The blue cheese part of the discs, between the vertebral bodies, acts as hydraulic ball bearings. When the vertebrae bend on each other, the nucleus pulposis and annular ligament acts as a hinge. It is a universal joint, like the ball joint in the front suspension of an automobile, allowing some rotation and tilting in all directions. The tough front part of the annulus fibrosis, along with a tough strap along the entire front of the spine, the anterior longitudinal ligament, locks this ball bearing chain of joints into alignment, and prevents one vertebra from sliding off the other one.

When the vertebrae tilt forward on one another, the arches separate and the ligaments of the arch stretch. When the body is bent backwards, these latter ligaments compress, and maintain the caliber and smooth contour of the spinal canal for the cord.

The portholes are made up like Babbott bearings, i.e.,
a complete foramen consists of half a hole in the
arch above and half in the arch below. Ordinarily
the holes are big enough to allow the nerves to go through
without being pinched or stretched. When the body bends
forewards, the portholes elongate into an oval, so that
the spinal cord and the roots can ride up slightly over
the curve made by the vertebral bodies. When one bends
backwards, these holes become shallower. At this point
the spinal cord is relaxed since it is on the inside of the
curve and the foramina compress and stabilize the roots
so that they do not become misplaced.

Like a good machine these actions go merrily on their way
for years. Totally unaware. Ignorance is bliss.
If this were all that there is to it, there would be no need
for this lecture.

We are supposed to talk about backache, which means
something is wrong. We must figure out what happens
to this beautiful mechanism that gives us so much
trouble before we cash in our chips.

We all know from experience that all manufactured products
are not put together properly. There is always a certain
percentage of lemons. Fix it up and make it usable. We
blame the lemons onto poor workmanship and inspection.
In the production of animals and human beings the same
phenomenon takes place. A certain percentage of us are
not put together right. Some of our parts are incomplete,
some are missing, some are fused together. We are born
that way. Who to blame except in heredity? Some of our genes
are programmed to produce abnormalities. Make the best & improve

7

6

About 15% of the general population has some type and degree of congenital malformation in the back. Most common, about 10%, is an incomplete fusion of the embryonic culvert, where the backbone and pelvis meet. 5th arch - gap. Usually does not cause trouble. A few cases also have a gap in the sacrum. The bigger the defect is, the more apt the patient is to have trouble. Missing bone is replaced by soft membrane. Too flexible to prevent strain + contusion of the underlying nerves when the back is injured. Spina bifida occulta. The worst form is spina bifida with meningocele. Some paralysis of legs, bowels, bladder. Hydrocephalus often associated with it. Brain + spinal cord float in cerebrospinal fluid.

Absence of whole or part of a vertebra. Messes up synchronization of the back. More prominent on maturity.

Also abnormal fusion in back where joints and ligaments are missing. More often in neck and tail end of the spine. Usually do not cause pain, but limit motion a bit throughout life. Easily adapted to.

Developmental deformities are more common than congenital. Localized abnormal growth. Several somites or single one. Usually hereditary. Scoliosis is the worst of these. (Describe) Secondary curve to keep eyes level & horizon. 12 years of age. Twisting is produced → hump + sunken breast. Many degrees, but majority are mild.
Kyphosis + lordosis. Sometimes hereditary. Also as a result of disease. Implications are mechanical from imbalance and impaired chest expansion. Strains easily → pain. Pain more chronic in older persons.

Wedged single vertebrae, narrow disc spaces (L5). All narrow disc spaces by X-ray do not signify injury.

Spondylolisthesis - mechanism of arch, slipping of body forward 4th, 5th, where most weight + motion are. Ligaments alone hold the spine together. Pain in low back + buttocks, not legs. Nerve not stretched

141

Symptomatic in pregnant women in 20's, men in their 30's. May never be symptomatic.

We have been talking about the slow, longstanding troubles of the back. Now we will focus our attention on the quick, destructive, more serious diseases. Inflammatory, infectious, neoplastic, degenerative, metabolic & miscellaneous.

(Inflammation (not necessarily infection). Rheumatoid arthritis (destructive to bone) is a severe back problem. Limbs & spine not in same patient. In spine → pain, weakness, gradually bending forward and eventually stiffening. Several years to burn out, but leaves its mark. Flexion is the worst result.

Childhood & adolescence - osteochondritis. All degrees.

Bacteria can invade and destroy any part of the body, including the spine. Tuberculosis → destruction & repair by fusion. Osteomyelitis & Infection of the discs. Meningitis. Fungi.

We are discussing the causes of back pain which make it wise to investigate prolonged pain and that which appears for no known reason. The earlier the cause is found the safer the patient should be. There is always a chance that there is a visitor in the woodpile or a tumor in the bone pile.

There are benign tumors which start in the backbone and are usually painful. Cannot escape detection if they are searched for. Malignant disease of the spine has a dreary outlook. Primary cancers of back (bones, muscle or nerve) are rare. Most of the spinal malignant diseases are metastatic. Prostate & breast notorious for this. Multiple myeloma is one of the most painful. Cancer of blood forming organs (bone marrow). Takes awhile to make the diagnosis.

If we live long enough, we all have degenerative disease of the spine. Wear & tear, break & mend, accompanies daily living. Mini trauma. Repair → hypertrophy & spurs, ridges, calcification of ligaments. Shrinking of nucleus pulposis. Vertebrae settle and we lose status after middle age.

This is the familiar _hypertrophic osteoarthritis_. Gradual loss of motion and stiffening over a period of years. (Degeneration of the spine).

Rheumatoid arthritis destroys bone and replaces it with either nothing or with fibrous tissue. This can cripple one in a hurry, early in life.

In this age of fads backache often is diagnosed "slipped disc." When I was growing up it was "sacro-iliac." Then one of my old professors in Boston discovered that the disc can also degenerate and bulge against the spinal cord and nerve roots. Sacro-iliac joint now takes a **back seat** (pun)

The ratio of elastic to fibrous tissue changes as we get older. Begin to stiffen up in 30's (professional athletes wear out). Our disc mechanisms begin to fall apart. Annulus fibrosis more subject to injury from strain, especially in the thinner part toward the cord. Bulging & tearing from flexion of the spine. The drier, harder nucleus pushes hard against the A.L and bulges it into the canal. Can happen in youth with more serious injuries. Space occupying lesions in the spinal canal produce trouble. Pressure, pinching against nerve root causes pain, weakness & numbness along the whole path of the affected nerve. Arms or legs are affected because HNP happens at ends of the spine. Causes topical symptoms in limb, not complete limb paralysis, pain or weakness. Exaggeration of reporting symptoms means something else is wrong (circulation?) or you have a good imagination. Bulging vs. blow out of N.P. Surgery for blow-out. 85% of bulging discs get better without surgery if given a chance.

Anatomy suggests that bulging discs are not the _only_ cause of nerve root pain. Anything that takes up space in the canal or port holes will pinch nerves. The disc is only one quarter of the circumference of the foramen. The rest is the apophyseal joints which can spur and ligamentum flavum which can become enlarged. I believe the disc gets blamed for more devilment than it deserves!

There are also metabolic diseases which affect the spine. Osteoporosis in old people. Sudden in women a few years after menopause. Protein matrix diminishes and bones become more porous and brittle. Painful for some reason. Subject to fractures more easily than at any other time of life. Causes kyphosis. Grandpop ties shoes, crushes vertebra. Old springs are getting weak and one of them busted when he bent over. Will heal in spite of Grandpop's age. Grandma's smaller bones may crush spontaneously. Disuse osteoporosis also. Bones remain healthy only when they are used.

Gout can affect the back as well as the big toe.

Injury: the struggle of the body against other objects. Most common in younger people because of greater and more dangerous activities. Fractures & dislocations of the spine – we have no choice but to be treated by the surgeon.

Most common of all causes of backaches are *sprains and strains*. Anatomy reveals the multiple reasons for misery in such a complex mechanism. Any of the structures can become overstretched, compressed, torn or bruised. I believe that most sudden low back pains are from muscle and ligament ~~sprain~~ strains. (Sprain means joint). No muscle in the body works alone – everything is synchronized. We are wired that way (nerve supply interconnections). The chain reaction is automatic. If one car jumps the track, the whole train is shaken up. Small muscles or ligaments tear a little bit away from the bone. Numb at first. After a few hours, swelling, stiffness, pain appear. The most common place for this is at the angle between the spine and pelvic bone, on the right side. This pain stays localized and is aggravated by certain motions of the body. Outside the spinal canal and roots.

Many of the buttock and leg pains are strains of the hip muscles of the thigh. The buttocks are actually part of the legs, but we think of them as the back.

Since the sciatic nerve goes down between these muscles there are usually some nerve symptoms which simulate slipped disc disease.

One of the most difficult parts of orthopedics is to distinguish one of these from the other. If one can find the culprit, one can take appropriate measures. If one cannot our efforts are less rewarding.

The back can also be destroyed from abnormal force through or outside the back, such as gunshot injuries. P.T. has no choice here, either.

We cannot blame all our troubles on something or somebody else. There is the by-a-bee of abuse. (abnormal use). Underuse of back → weakness, obesity, poor coordination. Overuse → osteo. or traumatic arthritis and chronic strains and sprains. Wrong posture, poor habits keeps the back aggravated by the diseases we have mentioned. If we are crazy enough, we are bound to get into trouble!

One of the big things that happens to our back is that we get old. Bones get softer → pain and fracture. We lose calcium + protein, the bones come closer together, motion is limited. Why do not all of our nerve roots get pinched when our discs dry up and get thinner? The ligaments also stiffen and shorten, and there is less motion. The body adjusts to the over the hill situation. Many of the problems of the aging back will settle down in time because of adaptability. The worst thing is to wait for nature to take care of things herself.

Back pains can also be caused by disease of the abdomen, chest, shoulders or hips. Outside aggravation of nerves, and muscles. See general physician first. In the woods we see individual trees and not the woods. (Specialist too soon!) If the family doctor cannot help you, let the orthopedist go out on the limb!

Why does the back ache? Bones themselves are insensitive. The soft tissues associated with the bones ache. Nerve endings in all the soft tissues. Of the back mechanism. Affected tissue swells and causes pressure on little nerve endings. Sensations → brain → muscles (spasm). Pain is a function of the nerves, which act as mediators between the injury and the repair process. It is no wonder that some of our pains are imaginary or psychological. If the irritation is in the local muscles of the back, the pain is apt to stay in the back. If the involvement is in the anterior branches the pain will be in the limbs and buttocks, rather than in the back.

Adam & Eve had computers on board. Memory is storage of impressions and recall of them over a lifetime. We remember our bad pains. Thankfully we do not have to push the recall button very often. Flu activates the pain memory bank. Depression, stress → play with the keyboard and mess around with the memory banks. Recall an old misery and put it to use to give us some relief from the real situation. Psychosomatic medicine, psychogenic overlay, hypochondria, "Compensationitis" and malingering. We can play the keyboard anyway we wish and if we are expert enough we can fool everybody, especially the orthopaedist. If we can be compensated emotionally, physically or financially the temptation to finger the keyboard is very strong. Easy compensation laws make compensationitis a serious problem. Partly a matter of morality, but not completely. Sometimes we get carried away and actually believe we are much worse off than we really are. Egged on by lawyers, family, friends — the world owes us a living for the alleged deep trouble we are in. At times we need psychological attention if we are off the beaten path a bit. We are not nuts but sometimes we need the head shrinker to find out whether we are really hurt or not.

What can we do about backache?

First - listen to the cry of the body for a breather. (Refuel, reload)

After injury - First take intensive rest for a short period. Let body adjust to the new situation without extra demands. Go to bed! If this does not work, seek help. In the hospital you rest.

Medication has been around since the beginning of time. Some cure, others mask.

Antiinflammatory drugs (aspirin, cortisone, butazolidin, etc.) act as fire extinguishers. They assist the body in curing the inflammation. Put the fire out. Pain is the smoke. Get rid of the smoke, but also put the fire out. Analgesics help inflammation and dull pain. Dope (narcotics) blow the smoke away but does nothing to put out the fire. Leads to dope addiction, partly because of imaginary pain. May be iatrogenic. Let the doctor handle the narcotics. Addiction → hurting yourself and losing credibility.

Exercise is necessary throughout life, and after injury, to keep the machine going. Aids circulation. Releases abnormal physical and mental tension.

Physiotherapy & exercise improve circulation. Forced physical training and healing response. Needed most in older, more indolent, people.

Manipulation (osteopathic & chiropractic) is a form of therapy. Acupuncture probably slows down the overactive memory bank for pain.

Braces & other supports have their place, usually temporarily, but sometimes permanently.

Surgery: Truly ruptured disc needs to be removed. Abscesses drained, unstable backs fused, severe scoliosis fused, some fractures & dislocations internally fixed and grafted, tumors removed. As a rule, if surgery is indicated, the sooner it is done, the better. Be conservative for awhile if possible.

These points require fine judgement of the physician, and are not easy for him, either.

How can we protect our backs?

Respect our age.

Youth - avoid abuse. We are not born with brains, and by the time we develop them we have done some pretty crazy things.

Older age - Slow down, but don't stop! Maintain muscle tone & correct posture all our lives. (Basic maintenance)

Combination of work and fun, not either one exclusively.

Control body weight. I'm the pot and you're the kettle, and I'm calling you black.

Underweight = poor mass and strength - neurasthenic.
Overweight = abnormal strain and fatigue.

Correct occupational and recreational habits. Use expert, skilled techniques. Don't blow it! Example: Overbalanced crane. Lift load correctly. Playpen, opening window. Trusting in sports dangerous. Don't spoil the music by sour notes from the orchestra. Sports equipment.

What else is needed? Prognosis?

Metric pain machine. - Electronic. Fought tooth and nail as an invasion of human rights. Aid diagnosis & prognosis. Screw up the compensation industry. Like dynamometer & lie detector, only better.

Improved patient acceptance of psychological therapy.

Improved attitude about compensation - pts, lawyers, third party.

Do not abuse insurance. Increased premiums.

Compensation is busy work for the lawyers. What are those poor guys going to do if we sue less?

Ways to put heat back into the old furnace. We hate to get old.

Best way is the idea conveyed in this last illustration.

M_____, M.D. 10/9/80

148

Fig. 1

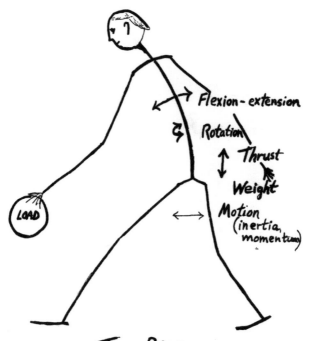

Flexion - extension

Rotation

Thrust

Weight

Motion
(inertia,
momentum)

LOAD

THE BACK
Keel, center of force and motion,
flexible positioner of the limbs.

Fig. 3

THE SOMITES
Why back problems affect
the limbs

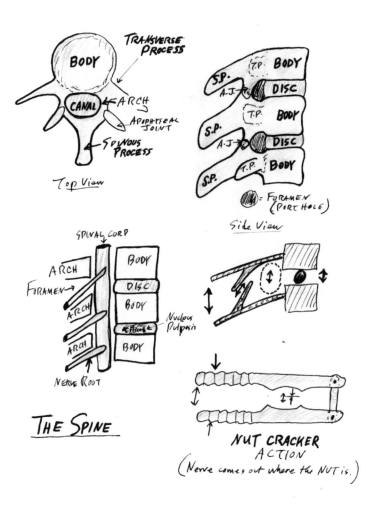

TRANSVERSE PROCESS

BODY

CANAL — ARCH

APOPHYSEAL JOINT

SPINOUS PROCESS

Top View

S.P.   T.P.   BODY
A.J.   DISC

T.P.   BODY
S.P.
A.J.   DISC

S.P.   T.P.   BODY

= FORAMEN (PORT HOLE)

Side View

SPINAL CORD

ARCH   BODY
FORAMEN →   DISC
ARCH   BODY
ARCH   Nucleus Pulposis
              BODY
NERVE ROOT

THE SPINE

NUT CRACKER
ACTION
(Nerve comes out where the NUT is.)

Fig. 5

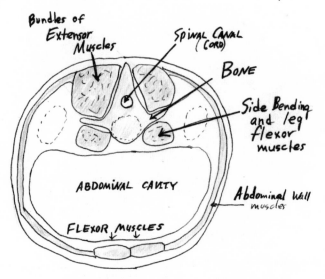

Bundles of
Extensor
Muscles

SPINAL CANAL
(CORD)

BONE

Side Bending
and leg
flexor
muscles

ABDOMINAL CAVITY

Abdominal Wall
muscles

FLEXOR MUSCLES

THE SPINAL MUSCLES
(CROSS SECTION)

Fig. 6

ABNORMALITIES

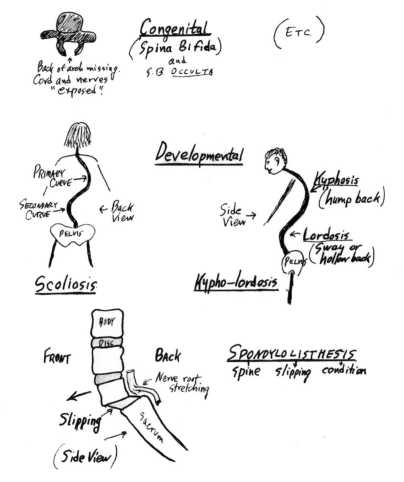

Back of arch missing.
Cord and nerves
"exposed".

Congenital
(Spina Bifida)
and
S.B. OCCULTA

(ETC.)

PRIMARY CURVE
SECONDARY CURVE
PELVIS
← Back View

Scoliosis

Developmental

Side View →

Kyphosis (hump back)

Lordosis (sway or hollow back)

PELVIS

Kypho-lordosis

BODY
DISC

FRONT

BACK

Nerve root stretching

Slipping

Sacrum

(Side View)

SPONDYLOLISTHESIS
spine slipping condition

153

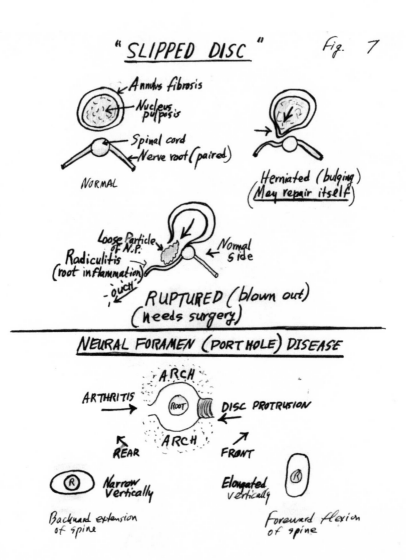

"*SLIPPED DISC*"   Fig. 7

Annulus fibrosis

Nucleus pulposis

Spinal cord

Nerve root (paired)

NORMAL

Herniated (bulging)
(May repair itself)

Loose Particle of N.P.

Radiculitis
(root inflammation)

Normal side

- ouch!

RUPTURED (blown out)
(needs surgery)

NEURAL FORAMEN (PORTHOLE) DISEASE

A.RCH

ARTHRITIS

ROOT

DISC PROTRUSION

ARCH

REAR   FRONT

R   Narrow Vertically

Elongated vertically   R

Backward extension of spine

Forward flexion of spine

154

THE CHAIN OF TROUBLE — Fig. 8

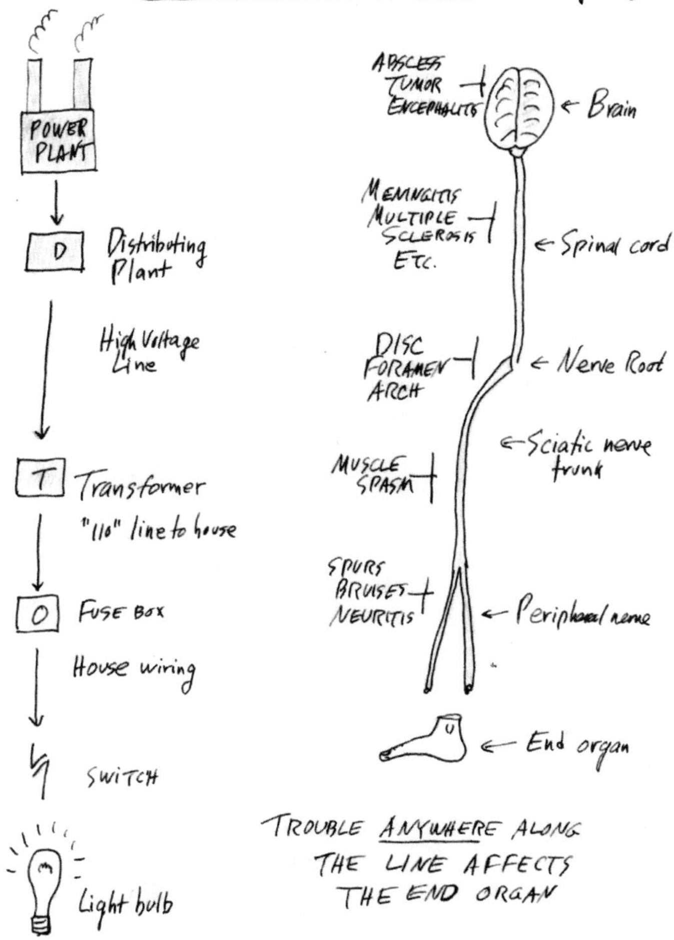

POWER PLANT

D — Distributing Plant

High Voltage Line

T — Transformer

"110" line to house

O — FUSE BOX

House wiring

SWITCH

Light bulb

ABSCESS
TUMOR
ENCEPHALITIS — ← Brain

MENINGITIS
MULTIPLE
SCLEROSIS
ETC. — ← Spinal cord

DISC
FORAMEN
ARCH — ← Nerve Root

← Sciatic nerve trunk

MUSCLE SPASM —

SPURS
BRUISES
NEURITIS — ← Peripheral nerve

← End organ

TROUBLE ANYWHERE ALONG THE LINE AFFECTS THE END ORGAN

BALDWIN 5-5756

JOHN ROYAL MOORE. M. D.
3701 NORTH BROAD STREET
PHILADELPHIA. PA. 19140

October 16, 1974

Morris A. Robbins M.D.
313 West Broad Street
Burlington, New Jersey 08016

Dear Morris: Re: Theodore Coffin

This note confirms the one dictated on the chart
at the time of our evaluation.

All evidence supports the concept that this is
an osteoma and for the pain to persist following
excision implies that there may have been one or
more nidi (have never observed one nor read about
it) or that part of the original nidus must still
exist. The proximity to the sacroiliac joint
could also account for the pain.

A laminograph of the sacroiliac joint, standing
x-ray of the pelvis, standing on the right leg and
then on the left with a 5 lb. weight on the free
leg (Chamberlain technique) may give additional
information as to the stability of this joint and
as to the localization of the present pain. Lateral
compression of the pelvis caused pain in the sacro-
iliac joint atea (also present in lateral recumbency)
on left leg standing.

The decision as to treatment may hinge on this
information. A sacroiliac arthrodesis may be
mandatory or complete exdision of the sclerotic
area. If the joint is unstabile, then fusion of
the symphysis and opposite sacroiliac joint will
have to be considered for pelvic stability.

With many thanks, I am

                          Sincerely yours,

JRM:F   J.R. Moore M.D.

cc: Mr. R.J. Wald Claim Supervisor

The Luncheon was great and the hospitality just the very very best — My love to you both
John Moore

Dr. John Royal Moore (1899-1988) was a pioneer of orthopedic surgery,
and Doc respected him very much. He founded the Temple University
Department of Orthopaedics and Sports Medicine. When Doc needed a
second opinion to back him up in an insurance claim, he went right to the top.

May 15, 1992

Morris A. Robbins, M.D.
313 West Broad Street
Burlington, New Jersey 08016

Dear Dr. Robbins:

Thank you for taking the time to forward further revisions of your national health reform report. I am sure that this information will be helpful in my consideration of legislative proposals in this area.

Please do not hesitate to contact me again on other matters of concern. I value your opinions and those of your fellow professionals.

Best wishes.

Sincerely,

Bill Bradley
United States Senator

BB/jsz

Doc shared his ideas with political leaders like Sen. Bill Bradley, Gov. Christie Whitman, and President Gerald Ford.

New age makes the new doctor's office impersonal

Why is it so complicated and difficult to visit and talk to a doctor today?

Older people remember their former physicians as accessible, patient and not condescending, and visits could resemble a religious experience. A medical office was private and dedicated to one practitioner and his patients. Confidentiality was not compromised by requests from third party insurers or attorneys. Diagnosis and therapy depended upon the doctor's knowledge, carefulness and judgment. Results were usually accepted as maximal.

In contrast, long waits for appointments, department store-like medical office complexes, overwhelming numbers of office assistants, computers, audible telephone conversations, white uniforms, forms to fill out for insurance and medical history, cubbyhole examining and treatment rooms containing patients waiting for the doctor to barge through, seemingly cursory examinations and snap judgments, impatience with questions and stinginess with alloted time for the patient make the visit rather unpleasant today.

What are the reasons for these changes?

The most obvious one is the urbanization and overwhelming numbers of patients. Doctors, most of whom are specialists, have cascaded and settled into groups practicing in hugh office complexes. Such offices must operate for efficiency, free traffic flow, large numbers of patients, adherence to regulations from many sources and profitability. Reams of paper work and reports to third parties necessitate the big front business office.

The second reason is the ever increasing complexity of diagnostic and treatment modalities which displace and replace the intimate doctor-patient relationship. The tendency is to treat the tests rather than the patient, or so it seems. Even if doctors took the time to explain the situation, the tests results would confuse the patient, they are so technical.

The third reason even displeases the doctor. It is the absolute necessity of practicing defensive medicine. People are litigation happy, although they may verbally deny it. The doctor's judgment is no longer enough. Expensive, usually unnecessary diagnostic tests are employed to rule out long shot possibilities that the doctor is wrong. An untested judgmental error results in a nasty lawsuit. Insurance premiums are extremely high for this reason, among others.

A fourth contributing factor is the medical entrepreneur who manages a department store of diagnostic and therapeutic machinery to extract all the profit the traffic will bear. This setup is a favorite place for the plaintiff lawyer to refer clients. Cross-consultations are the rule, to amplify the situation. Naturally, these environments add to the complexity and inconvenience that patients experience. These "health industries" do not let the patient go until they are forced to.

A fifth difficulty has been added recently. HMO and other captive health plans make it mandatory to go to the participating doctor. Appointments are crowded. Waiting time is prolonged as the busy doctor is usually not on time. The primary physician must see the patient first to allow the assigned health plan specialist into the picture. Then the appointment-and-waiting process is repeated.

We all wish things were more like they used to be. This is out of the question and the past is unrecoverable history.

M.A. Robbins, M.D.
Burlington City

Sunday, November 17, 1991

Burlington County Times

Reprinted with permission: Burlington County Times

Doc Robbins

by Dorothy Robbins Talavera
Reprinted with permission: Published in the Beverly Bee, October 2020, VOL.XXII issue 10, pages 24-25

Raise your hand if you or someone you know was a patient of Dr. Morris A. Robbins. Doc was a one-armed orthopedic surgeon who practiced in South Jersey for 50 years. Yes. A one-armed surgeon! The question asked over and over is "what happened to his arm?"

Morris was raised in tiny Jacksonville, New Jersey. The family lived right next-door to the church, where his mother was the organist. His father was a union carpenter who built some of the barracks at Fort Dix. He was a good student, a Boy Scout, enthusiastic YMCA member, and a violinist in the Mount Holly High School orchestra. He was editor-in-chief of the school paper, an expert on the local Native Americans, and a public speaker. With this background, he was easily accepted into college. His plan was to study pre-med, then go on to become a surgeon. Then, life changed forever.

On a rainy evening in 1935 he was driving his girlfriend home from a last date before going off to college, when they came upon the scene of an auto accident. In those days, the law required passers-by to stop and lend aid. Robbins stepped out of his car into the wet grass, not realizing the accident had knocked down a high tension overhead electric wire. Instantly, he was electrocuted, with third-degree burns over most of his body. He was not expected to live the night.

For the next three years, Robbins was in and out of long hospital stays. He underwent fifteen operations. His left arm was so badly damaged, it had to be amputated just below the elbow. The pain was excruciating: the exposed nerves in his arm, daily removal of dead tissue, skin grafts, and more. His remaining hand was covered in so much scar tissue, it had limited flexibility. In his memoir, The Life and Times of a One-Armed Surgeon[35], he wrote about that period in his life: *During my convalescence I realized that the world had suddenly become hostile to me. ...(people) acted horrified at my appearance. I had to learn to do everything over again"*

A commercial artificial arm Robbins bought was not satisfactory. Always a tinkerer, he began designing and constructing a constantly evolving series of protheses that allowed dexterity of movement, including moving fingers. For the rest of his life, he worked on improvements in his arm and hands. Wood, fiberglass, rubber bands, and nylon fishing line were the main ingredients. Different arms had different purposes.

Finally, he was well enough to start college. This time, he decided to commute to the University of Pennsylvania, instead of the far away school to which he originally was accepted. Robbins worked hard, putting in many extra hours. He deliberately took the most meticulous dissecting labs to prove he could do it with his damaged hands. He earned the highest comprehensive grade in his zoology major that anyone had attained in the previous ten years, and graduated with Major Honors. He felt ready to apply to Penn's medical school.

"*Now my troubles recurred. None of the five medical schools in Philadelphia would even interview me. Penn said the student health department rejected me. I had the same experience with schools in ... other major cities,*"[36] he recalled. In a 1990 interview with the Burlington County Times; Doc recounted what his office staff called "the Miracles". As reported in the article: "*He hoped to go to the University of Virginia. And on the way south, he and a pal got stuck in traffic in Baltimore. 'I looked up, and there was the medical school of the University of Maryland." Robbins said. ... I got out and I went in there. I fumbled around and I found a back elevator. There was a sign on there 'Students not allowed to use the elevator.' Well, I wasn't a student. But I couldn't get the damned thing to run. So, this bald-headed man comes along,*

---

35   Life and Times of a One-Armed Surgeon by Morris A. Robbins, M.D.

36   Robbins, p. 36.

says 'Can I help you?' I said, 'Yeah, I want to up to the dean's office.' He said, 'All right, let's go' "He goes up, puts me in the dean's office, and goes around the other side of the desk and said, 'What can I do for you?' "Good grief. The dean himself. "In 15 minutes, I was accepted –without any papers." Robbins said. The dean saw the homemade prosthesis, along with Robbins creativity and determination. He didn't even ask how a man with hands like that could become a doctor. He knew he'd find a way. "He said, 'There's a place for you in medicine. You're in!' "Robbins said.[37]

So, Robbins settled into the Baltimore campus, and threw himself wholeheartedly into his studies. In his memoir he writes, "*our classes were mobilized because of World War II activities. All of the fellows were put in uniform, and were paid by the government. I was 4-F[38], of course, and still a civilian.*" Once again, his hard work was noticed. His mother, Sarah Robbins, wrote about attending his medical school graduation in a letter to a relative: "*When he went up to get his diploma was another big moment. The big high man of the class with the highest mark was applauded all the way to his seat. And when it came to Morris, they did the same thing for him.*"[39]

Robbins interned at Cooper Hospital in Camden. His mentor and supporter was Dr. Benjamin Franklin Buzby, the doctor who had saved his life in 1935.

In 1945, Dr. Robbins married his sweetheart Betty Sutton, and took over the practice vacated by Dr Arthur Peacock in Columbus, NJ. His office was in a section of their house on Main Street. Soon, the family was joined by two children, Dorothy and Bill.

For many years, Doc was the country doctor for the small, rural village. Patients flocked to his office, with or without appointments; he made house calls, delivered babies at home, and dispensed medicines because the nearest pharmacy was in Mount Holly. Privacy concerns were different in those days, and the local newspapers reported every instance of" So-and-so is recovering from stomach trouble, under the care of Dr. Morris Robbins."

---

37   "Special man became surgeon his way" By Jack Knarr, <u>Burlington County Times</u>, Wednesday, December 19, 1990

38   In the days of Selective Service and the draft, a designation of 4-F indicated that the man was rejected for military service, due to medical or other disqualifying reasons.

39   Letter from Sarah Robbins, Jacksonville, NJ, Oct. 6, 1944

But surgery was his dream. So, in 1955 he began a new residency at the Hospital for Crippled Children in Newark to study orthopedic surgery. He took on a young partner, Dr. Lawrence McCay, to run the practice while he was away. Betty started a teaching position in New Hanover Township to support the family.

Another frequently asked question is, "How did you end up in Delanco?" One day, the Robbins received a bombshell. Here is how Doc described it in his memoir: *"On June 26, 1956...I was notified by the New Jersey State Highway Commission that my property in Columbus stands in the way of the proposed new Route 206, and that I must vacate by September 30 1956."*[40] With Doc spending his week in Newark, Betty teaching full time, and 2 young children, there was no luxury to go house-hunting. They had to close out the medical practice, find somewhere affordable to live on a teacher's salary, get all the paperwork completed and move within a 3-month window!

Dr. McCay told Doc that his father, State Senator Albert McCay, had just moved with his wife Grace and son Bob to Delanco, and the small house next-door was for sale. So, Doc and Betty bought it.

Once the crisis had passed, and the advanced training was completed, Doc's new practice flourished. For the next four decades, he saw patients at his Burlington office, Zurbrugg Hospital in Riverside, and Memorial Hospital in Mount Holly. He also was asked to join the staff of Burdette Tomlin Hospital in Hammonton and Memorial Hospital in Cape May Court House. Even today, twenty-five years after he retired, his patients still talk about him. He was accessible, he listened to people, and he cared about them. In a recent conversation with a group of people that included a former patient., someone asked "Didn't you feel uncomfortable being operated on by a doctor with only one arm?" The former patient replied, "No. Everybody knew he was the best."

Despite a grueling work schedule, Doc was a popular public speaker, contributor to a regular medical advice column in the Burlington County Times, author of medical journal articles, president of the Burlington County Medical Society, and inventor. One passion was designing vehicles and devices that would allow paralyzed individuals to live more independently. His inspiration – once again – came from the McCays. Bob McCay had been confined to a wheelchair since he was a teenager.

---

40   Robbins, page 69

Many people around Burlington County recognized Doc for the vehicles he drove. Back when he was driving to Newark, he needed to replace his aging Studebaker with something reliable and efficient. He bought a new (1956) Thunderbird convertible, which has been in the family ever since. Once he started twice weekly trips to Hammonton and Cape May Court House in all kinds of weather, leaving and returning home in the dark, he bought the first of his 4-wheel-drive Ford Broncos. Finally, after retirement, he made daily rounds of the streets of Delanco on his adult-size tricycle for exercise.

After his death in 2004, his adopted town of Delanco honored Doc's life and work by naming a street near his home Robbins Lane. Doc Robbins was one of a kind. They don't make doctors like him anymore.

Index

Department of Occupational Health 102

E

Edwards, Dr. Charles Reid 50

F

Fishbein, Dr. Morris 40
Ford, President Gerald 158
Franklin Institute 39

G

Gamon, Dr. Robert 56
George, Dr. Amerigo 95
Grant, Dr. Ward 50
Greene, Dr. Lloyd B. 68

H

Haines, Mary 29
Hammonton, New Jersey 95
Heal, Dr. Robert 108
Holbein, Francis W. 17, 24
Hospital for Crippled Children 81

I

Interstate Tugboat Transporter 81, 100

J

Jacksonville, New Jersey 6, 7

K

Kekevat, Dr. Hassan 96
Kessler, Dr. Henry 81, 83
Kessler Institute for Rehabilitation 81
Kessler Memorial Hospital 95, 123
Kirk, Dr. Norman T. 51

L

Lupton, Capt. Chris 100

M

March of Dimes 82
Martin, Glenn L. 46

U

United Mine Workers 83
University of Maryland 41
University of Pennsylvania 36, 37
University of Pennsylvania Graduate School of Medicine 83
University of Virginia 40

V

Viteri, Dr. Luis 77

W

Whitman, Gov. Christie 158
Willingboro New Jersey 97
World War II 115
Wylie, Dr. H. Boyd 43

Y

Y.M.C.A. 16, 18, 24, 35, 37

Z

Zurbrugg Memorial Hospital 92, 102, 123

Morris A. Robbins, M.D.
picture taken for the University of Maryland School of Medicine, Graduating
Class 1944.